Studies in Christian Philosophy

A Virtue Ethical View of Trinitarian Sanctification, Ronald M. Rothenberg
Omniscience, Foreknowledge, and the Problem of Divine Freedom, Graham Floyd

Omniscience, Foreknowledge, and the Problem of Divine Freedom

Omniscience, Foreknowledge, and the Problem of Divine Freedom

Graham Corbett Floyd

Fontes

Omniscience, Foreknowledge, and the Problem of Divine Freedom

Copyright © 2019 by Graham Corbett Floyd

ISBN-13: 978-1-948048-10-1 (hardback)
ISBN-13: 978-1-948048-11-8 (paperback)

All rights reserved. No part of this publication may be reproduced, stored in a retrieval system, or transmitted in any form or by any means—electronic, mechanical, photocopy, recording, or any other—except for brief quotations in printed reviews, without the prior permission of the publisher.

FONTES PRESS
DALLAS, TX
www.fontespress.com

Contents

Abbreviations ix
Introduction 1

1. Omniscience 7
   God and Abstract Entities 8
   Uncreated vs. Created Abstract Entities 9
   Criticism of Created Abstract Entities and Nominalism 14
   Assessment 20
   Defining Omniscience 21
       Essential Property 21
       Scope 27
       Unchangeable 28
       Creative and Modal 31
       The Future 32
   Conclusion 33

2. The Problem of Divine Freedom 35
   Defining Freedom 36
   The Problem 38
       Pike's Argument 38
       Zagzebski's Argument 40
   Examining Divine Freedom 43
   Assessment 51

3. The Open Solution 55
   The Open View of the Future 55
   Versions of the Open View 59
       Voluntary Nescience 60
       Involuntary Nescience 62
       Non-Bivalent Omniscience 65
       Bivalent Omniscience 68
   Assessing the Theories 71
   Divine Freedom and Bivalent Omniscience 76
   Conclusion 80

4. The Molinist Solution 83
   Molinism 83
   Knowledge of Counterfactuals of Freedom 87
   Choosing a Method of Knowing 90
   Divine Freedom and the Molinist Solution 93
   Conclusion 101

5. The Ockhamist Solution 103
   Ockham's Solution 103
   Modern Interpretations 107

  The Hard-Soft Fact Distinction 107
  Power Over the Past 112
 Divine Freedom and the Ockhamist Solution............................. 114
 Conclusion 122

6. THE ATEMPORAL SOLUTION... 123
 Atemporalism... 123
 Assessment of the Atemporal Solution..................................... 129
  Implications for Divine Freedom 129
  An Atemporal Understanding of Divine Freedom....................... 133
 Criticisms of the Atemporal Solution 138
 Conclusion 148

BIBLIOGRAPHY.. 151

ABBREVIATIONS

APQ	American Philosophical Quarterly
ATJ	Ashland Theological Journal
CJP	Canadian Journal of Philosophy
EJPR	European Journal for Philosophy of Religion
FP	Faith and Philosophy
IJPR	International Journal for Philosophy of Religion
JAAR	Journal of the American Academy of Religion
JBS	Journal of Biblical Studies
JETS	Journal of the Evangelical Theological Society
JP	Journal of Philosophy
PAAPA	Proceedings and Addresses of the American Philosophical Association
PACPA	Proceedings of the American Catholic Philosophical Association
PC	Philosophia Christi
POS	Philosophy of Science
PP	Philosophical Perspectives
PPQ	Pacific Philosophical Quarterly
PPR	Philosophy and Phenomenological Research
PQ	Philosophical Quarterly
PR	Philosophical Review

PRS	*Perspectives in Religious Studies*
PS	*Philosophical Studies*
PT	*Philosophy and Theology*
RM	*The Review of Metaphysics*
RS	*Religious Studies*
SWJT	*Southwestern Journal of Theology*
SVTQ	*St. Vladimir's Theological Quarterly*
WTJ	*Wesleyan Theological Journal*

Introduction

Philosophy of religion has long dealt with the problem regarding the compatibility between divine foreknowledge and human freedom. The problem states that if God possesses knowledge of the future, then all human choices and actions are determined and must occur. They may not be other than what they are. If these choices and actions cannot be otherwise than what the divine knowledge stipulates, then human beings cannot possess freedom. Much ink has been spilled attempting to find a solution that upholds both the divine foreknowledge of the future and the human agent's ability to do otherwise, and the debate still rages over whether or not a successful solution has been devised.

While most philosophers are focused on the problem that foreknowledge poses for human freedom, I propose to look at this problem from another angle. If God possesses knowledge of the future, then it is not just the choices and actions of human beings that God foreknows. It would seem that he should also foreknow his own choices and actions. As a result, just as there is a concern regarding the compatibility of human freedom with foreknowledge, there is also a concern regarding the compatibility of divine freedom with foreknowledge. This study seeks to explore this issue and search for potential solutions to this problem. In the end, I argue that among current lines of thought on the issue of freedom and its compatibility with divine foreknowledge, there is only one that is capable of solving the divine free will dilemma. That view is the atemporal, Thomistic view. This view argues that God is an atemporal being who is not subject to time; therefore, there need not be any worry of God foreknowing his own act of will prior to actualizing that act of will. Since God acts in one atemporal moment, there is no time before his act in which God foreknows what he will do, nor is such knowledge essential to the divine being. Thus, the problem of the compatibility between foreknowledge and divine freedom may be avoided.

In chapter one, I will examine and define the divine property of omniscience since it plays a major role in the problem of freedom and foreknowledge in general. To begin, I argue that omniscience cannot be properly understood without first examining the issue of God's relationship to abstract entities, namely universals. I will argue that these entities are the foundation of God's knowledge and an essential part of the divine nature. They will play a major role in explaining what and how God knows, particularly his knowledge of the future. I contend that abstract entities are to be identified with the divine ideas themselves rather than as entities external to the divine being or created by God. I then examine the implications that such a theory has on the definition of omniscience. I argue that the theory of divine ideas is a great-making property that provides God with all knowledge immediately and without the need for learning making him essentially omniscient. I further argue that God's knowledge of the future of the temporal world is best characterized in terms of his knowledge of certain abstract entities, such as possible worlds, that exist within the divine mind. Since the divine ideas function as the essences of objects, such as possible worlds, and all objects participate with these ideas, God is able to know the effects of such objects as they reside within the object's essence. Thus, I argue that God does possess knowledge of all events and actions that occur in any possible world that may be instantiated.

In chapter two, I explore the implication of God's knowledge of the future by explicating the problem of foreknowledge and human freedom and demonstrating how it also can be applied to God. First, I define the two major types of freedom that an agent may possess. The first is freedom of indifference, also known as libertarian freedom. This version of freedom argues that an agent must be able to do otherwise in order to be considered free. The second is freedom of spontaneity, also known as compatibilist freedom. This version of freedom argues that an agent need not possess the ability to do otherwise but only need desire to do some action in order to be free. Second, I explicate two major arguments used to claim that divine foreknowledge robs agents of their freedom. The first is Nelson Pike's famous argument against the ability to alter the past beliefs of God. In this argument, Pike claims that since God knows what an agent will do prior to the agent's performing that action and that the agent is unable to alter what God foreknows, the agent is not free in his action. The second is Linda Zagzebski's argument from the accidental necessity of God's beliefs to the necessity of an agent's action. Since God's beliefs about the future are in the past or like the past in that they are now actual, these beliefs are now accidentally necessary and cannot be otherwise. Thus, whatever these beliefs imply must obtain, robbing agents of their freedom. I show how each of these arguments can subsequently be applied to God and his knowledge of his own actions such that it becomes questionable that God is a free being. After discussing some contemporary thought on the issue of God's freedom as it relates to his foreknowledge, I propose to examine the major solutions to the problem of foreknowledge and human freedom as a means of solving the problem of foreknowledge and divine freedom. I also propose a set of three criteria to be used as a means for determining a successful solution to the problem of divine freedom and foreknowledge. The first criterion is that logical fatalism must be avoided. God must not be logically necessitated to act a certain way. The second criterion is that natural necessity must be avoided. God must not be necessitated by his nature to act in a certain way. The third criterion is that any solution must be compatible with the theory of divine ideas and its implications regarding God's ability to know the future.

In chapter three, I begin the search for a successful solution by examining the Open Solution. This solution seeks to avoid the problem of foreknowledge and human freedom primarily by denying that God possesses knowledge of the future, particularly the actions of agents; for if he did, then the future would be determined and agents would not be free. Thus, the future is considered to be open and free. There are four different versions of the Open Solution: Voluntary Nescience, Involuntary Nescience, Bivalent Omniscience, and Non-Bivalent Omniscience. Voluntary Nescience argues that while God knows the future, he exercises the ability to forget or block such knowledge from his mind. Involuntary Nescience argues that while the future is settled, it is logically impossible that God possess such knowledge. Non-Bivalent Omniscience argues that bivalence is false and that propositions about the future do not possess a truth value making them unknowable. Bivalent Omniscience argues that all propositions have a truth value and that propositions about the future are false. I explain each theory and argue that Bivalent Omniscience is the best version of the position. Then, I apply the argument of Bivalent Omniscience to the problem of divine freedom and foreknowledge. I then offer criticisms of this view as a potential solution to the problem of divine freedom and foreknowledge. I conclude that this version of the Open Solution does not meet the three criteria for a successful solution to the problem of divine freedom.

In chapter four, I explore the Molinist Solution to the problem of foreknowledge and human freedom. This position argues that God possesses a special kind of knowledge called middle knowledge that allows him to know what free creatures would freely do in any circumstance. If God actualizes that circumstance, then God knows the future. This view also has several nuanced interpretations, particularly as it pertains to the method of grounding the truth of these counterfactuals of freedom. The first method is to ground counterfactuals in the essence of the agent. The second is to ground counterfactuals of freedom in the future occurrence of the action. The third is to ground counterfactuals of freedom in the actions of the agent himself. The fourth is to claim that counterfactuals of freedom are brute facts that do not need to be grounded. I argue that the brute fact method is the only option and apply the Molinist theory to the divine being with this understanding. After applying the Molinist view to the problem of foreknowledge and divine freedom, I provide reasons for believing that this view also fails to uphold the three criteria for a successful conclusion to the problem of divine freedom, and I reject it.

In chapter five, I take up the Ockhamist Solution as a potential solution to the problem of foreknowledge and divine freedom. This solution argues that while God does have foreknowledge, that knowledge is ultimately dependent upon future events for its truth. This dependence points to the existence of the logical possibility that things could be different and allows free agents some say in what will transpire. While there is really only one position, there are different ways of understanding this position that place emphasis on different aspects of the position. Ockham claims that while propositions about the future are true, they are contingently true or false. While they do possess a truth value, they could have possessed a different truth value. What ultimately determines this truth value is a future event, and God could have known differently up until the event obtains. Thus, the truth of God's foreknowledge is to some degree dependent on the future actions of agents who logically can do otherwise. If the agent would have done otherwise, God would have known otherwise. The Hard-Soft Fact distinction emphasizes Ockham's distinction between contingent and non-contingent propositions. Utilizing Ockham's notion of the truth of future propositions being conditionally determined by an agent's future actions, this position argues that propositions can be divided into hard facts whose truth value cannot be affected and soft facts whose truth value is conditioned by future events. Since propositions about the future are soft, they are contingently true or false as Ockham claims. Others focus on Ockham's notion that agents have a power over what

God believes, known as counterfactual power over the past, such that if they would have acted differently, then God would have known differently. I apply the Ockhamist Solution to the problem of foreknowledge and divine freedom. Like the solutions before it, I argue that the Ockhamist Solution fails to uphold the three criteria for a successful solution to the problem of foreknowledge and divine freedom, and it must be rejected.

In chapter six, I explore the Atemporal Solution as a potential means to solve the problem of foreknowledge and divine freedom. The atemporal solution holds that God is not a temporal being but exists outside the scope of temporal reality. The view was first applied to the problem of foreknowledge and human freedom by Boethius. He claimed that God embraces all of time in one eternal moment. Since all of time exists before God, he is able to view all of time at once. God, therefore, knows the future as actually occurring rather than as yet to occur. Thus, agents freely act and God observes how they freely act in his eternal state. There are two ways to understand the atemporal position. The first is to break God's eternal state down into three logically distinct moments that conceptually explain God's creation and observation of what he creates. In the first moment, God possesses his natural knowledge of all that is possible. In the second moment, God creatively acts. In the third moment, God possesses free knowledge of all that occurs within the temporal world. One concern with this position is that it implies that God is dependent on creation for what he knows. There are different ways of responding to this concern if one is not willing to embrace it. The first is to argue that an agent's action causally flows from his character, allowing God to know the action logically prior to the obtaining of the action. The other is to claim that God is able to guess with a high level of probability how the agent will act. A second way to understand the atemporal position is to argue that time is not created all at once but temporally proceeds along temporal points. God, however, timelessly knows the temporal world by consulting the divine ideas since the temporal world proceeds according to the divine ideas. As a result, God bears no relation to time other than to create it and sustain it.

After applying the atemporal position to the problem of foreknowledge and divine freedom, I engage a prominent argument against the atemporal position and its compatibility with freedom and apply it to divine freedom. I conclude that the only atemporal model that successfully avoids this criticism is the logical moments model. I then explicate and support the Thomistic model of divine freedom as compatible with the logical moments model and argue that it upholds all of the criteria for a successful solution to the problem of foreknowledge and divine freedom. I also defend the Thomistic model of divine freedom against several criticisms. Thus, I conclude that the Atemporal Solution utilizing the logical moments model of eternity and the Thomistic model of divine freedom is the only viable understanding of foreknowledge and its relationship with divine freedom.

CHAPTER 1

OMNISCIENCE

When looking at the proposed problem with foreknowledge and divine freedom, an examination of the divine property of omniscience must be undertaken. Since the foreknowledge-freedom problem is integrally tied to one's understanding of omniscience, the problem with divine freedom will also be affected by this doctrine. This chapter must determine what is the correct understanding and definition of divine omniscience. The Bible expresses several principles of the divine knowledge. First, the biblical authors state that God's knowledge is greater than that of humans. Second, the Bible states that God knows all about human beings both in general and specifically. Third, God's knowledge has great extent or great amount. God possesses far more knowledge than any human being is capable of ever possessing. Fourth, God's knowledge is perfect such that it encompasses all of reality. Lastly, God knows the future.[1] These principles offer a simple, biblical picture of the doctrine of omniscience.

Omniscience, however, is a much more complex doctrine than what these simple principles express. This chapter focuses on explicating the doctrine of omniscience and its complexities so that the problem of foreknowledge and divine freedom can be properly understood. The first section analyzes the metaphysical theories regarding God's relationship to abstract entities as the source and ground for God's omniscience. As an omniscient being, God always knows all truths. Since knowledge involves truth and it is assumed that truth corresponds to reality, what God knows must be grounded in a reality. Without a reality on which to ground God's knowledge, it is impossible for

---

[1] For extensive discussion on the relevant biblical texts, see Millard Erickson, *God the Father Almighty* (Baker Books, 1998), 186–189.

God to know anything. I conclude that the best explanation for grounding God's knowledge is the theory of divine ideas. The second section outlines various implications that such a theory of divine ideas has for the doctrine of omniscience, particularly the implication that God knows his own future. It is this understanding of omniscience that I will utilize for the rest of this study.

God and Abstract Entities

God is typically thought of as independent and self-sufficient, making him supremely sovereign over reality. This is traditionally referred to as God's aseity or as being *a se*: existing of and from oneself. All that is distinct from God is therefore dependent on his creative and sustaining activity. Paul Gould states that this concept can be expressed in the following proposition of Absolute Dependency:

> AD: God does not depend on anything distinct from Himself for His existing. Everything distinct from God depends on God's creative activity for its existing.[2]

This concept applies easily to the universe. God creates the universe, but he exists either logically or temporally prior to and independent of it. There is, however, one thing that seems to challenge this proposition: the necessary existence of abstract entities, namely universals.

Beginning with Plato, many philosophers have believed that certain abstract entities (Forms or universals) necessarily exist and provide the metaphysical basis for all of reality. The existence of such entities raises the question of God's relationship with these abstract objects, particularly since his sovereignty and knowledge would be intimately connected with them. Gould presents this conflict by introducing his Inconsistent Triad:

> (1) Abstract entities exist necessarily (Platonism).
> (2) Abstract entities distinct from God are created by God and hence dependent.
> (3) If abstract entities exist necessarily, they are either independent or uncreated.[3]

---

[2] Paul Gould, "The Problem of God and Abstract Objects," *PC* 13, no. 2 (2011): 256.
[3] Ibid., 257.

One of these three positions must be rejected. If God is dependent on these entities for his knowledge of reality, then it seems that God is dependent on something external to his being which he does not control.

The rejection of claim (2) is what Gould calls the Ultimacy Problem. Properties exist independently of God, and God essentially has properties. As a result, God's nature is derived or actualized by some other entity, namely abstract entities. God would then be dependent on something outside of himself for being who he is, making him dependent and subservient. God would not be the ultimate reality. The Platonic Theist (one who holds to 1 and 3) must admit this conclusion. On the other hand, the rejection of claim (3) raises questions concerning the dependency relation between God and abstract entities. How do these abstract entities depend upon God? The relation cannot be merely logical dependence where the existence of God entails the existence of abstract objects but abstract objects do not entail God's existence. The divine properties would exist logically prior to the abstract entities that ground them. Rather, it would be a mutual logical dependence where the existence of God entails the existence of abstract entities and vice versa. This implication, however, creates a further problem, which Gould calls the Dependency Problem.[4] Abstract entities would exist in the same *a se*, independent, and necessary manner as God. They would not need to depend on God for their existence; however, these abstract entities are supposed to be dependent on God for their existence since he is their creator. Thus, abstract entities may not be necessary but contingent. How then should this dependence relationship be understood? Should abstract entities be rejected altogether? How will this understanding affect the definition of divine omniscience?

Uncreated vs. Created Abstract Entities

As stated in the previous paragraph, the Platonic Theist rejects claim (2) and upholds the strong Platonic Theory of abstract entities.[5] A typical reason for

---

4 Ibid., 258.
5 Ibid., 261. For arguments in favor of Platonic Theism, see Roy Clouser, *The Myth of Religious Neutrality: An Essay on the Hidden Role of Religious Belief in Theories*, rev. ed. (University of Notre Dame Press, 2005); Peter van Inwagen, "A Theory of Properties," in *Oxford Studies in Metaphysics*, vol. 1, ed. Dean Zimmerman (Clarendon Press, 2005), 107–138; idem, "God and Other Created Things," in *Metaphysics and God: Essays in Honor of Eleonore Stump*, ed. Kevin Tempe (Routledge, 2009), 3–20; idem, "Relational vs. Constituent Ontologies," *PP* 25 (2011): 389–405; idem, "Did God Create Shapes?" *PC* 17, no. 2 (2015): 285–290.

Gould notes that there is a version of Platonic Theism, which he dubs Dependent Platonic Theism, which denies (3) instead of (2). Abstract objects are necessary, but they are created by God, separate from him, and dependent on him for their existence. A proponent of this view would be Rene Descartes. See Rene Descartes, *Oeuvres*, ed. C. Adam and P. Tammery (Paris:

this position is that propositions are claimed to be bearers of truth value because they are what sentences assert. Propositions are not sentences themselves, since the same proposition can be asserted by more than one sentence in both the same and different languages. Thus, propositions must be entities that exist independent of the mind. Platonic Theists contend that exegetical evidence, like Col 1:16–17, seems to indicate that both the visible and invisible realities are created by God, but this is questionable. Critics claim that it is unlikely that the biblical authors or the Church Fathers had metaphysics in mind when this passage was written, so one may infer that this passage does not apply to Platonic entities like propositions.[6] Also, Platonic Theists advocate the claim that theories involving created abstract entities do not provide adequate interpretations of the notions of creation and dependence. As a result, they do not show that there is an incompatibility between God's sovereignty and the existence of independent abstract entities. Thus, it is not evident that theories of the creation of abstract entities are simpler than Platonic theories. It is contended that the view of Platonic Theism can be entirely consistent with the theistic claim that God is sovereign and exists *a se*.[7]

Platonic Theism, however, seems to imply some unsettling consequences for God. Thomas Aquinas argues that if abstract entities reside external to God, then God would not have perfect intellect and would depend on something outside of himself in order to know.[8] If Aquinas' contention that abstract entities affect God's existence is true, then Platonic Theism seems to imply that God is not the ultimate source of all things. He is dependent on something other than himself. These concerns, however, might be easily sidestepped. If God necessarily exists and is necessarily omniscient, then God knows all things by nature. This implies that there is no need to worry about God being dependent on something else for his knowledge since he has his knowledge naturally. He does not incorporate knowledge into his mind. Even if abstract entities exist independently from God, he is still not dependent on anything and remains the ultimate source of all creation. Still, some theists

---

Vrin, 1964), I: 135,147, 151, III: 648, IV: 110, VII: 64, 80, 116–118, 383, 436, VIII: 380, XI: 37; idem, *Philosophical Works*, trans. E. Haldane and G. T. Ross (Cambridge University Press, 1967), I: 121, 192, II: 19–21, 226, 228, 251; idem, *Philosophical Letters*, trans. A. Kenny (Clarendon, 1970), 11, 13, 14, 136, 151; Anthony Kenny, *God of the Philosophers* (Oxford University Press, 1979), 17–22. Keith Yandell calls this position Theistic Emanationism. See Keith Yandell, "God and Propositions," *PC* 13 (2012): 283–284; idem, "God and Propositions," in *Beyond the Control of God?: Six Views on the Problem of God and Abstract Objects*, ed. Paul Gould (Bloomsbury, 2014), 30–33.

6 See Yandell, "God and Propositions," 276–77; idem, *Beyond the Control of God*, 26–30. Scott Davison, "Could Abstract Objects Depend Upon God?" *RS* 27 (1991): 485, 488–489.

7 Davison, "Abstract Objects," 490–496.

8 Thomas Aquinas, *Summa contra Gentiles*, vol. 1, trans. Anton Pegis (University of Notre Dame Press, 1975), 1.16.1–7, 1.51.4–6.

will be uncomfortable with such a relation between God and abstract entities. Would not God's necessary omniscience still depend on abstract entities as the ground for God's omniscient truth even if God does not incorporate knowledge into his mind? God could not know if abstract entities did not first establish what he can know. As a result, if there is an adequate way to avoid this relation, then it seems that Platonic Theism should be rejected.

A more troubling issue with Platonic Theism is that God's existence appears to be dependent on abstract entities. If abstract entities exist necessarily and uncreated by God, then abstract entities like *omnipotence, perfect goodness,* and *deity* exist necessarily and separately from God. God, however, is composed of these properties; therefore, God is dependent on these entities in order to be who he is. This implication appears to violate the doctrine of divine aseity where God exists independently and self-sufficiently of any other thing.[9] As a result, Platonic Theism appears to remove God's status as the highest of all ontological beings and make him subservient to a higher reality.

Having understood this dependency issue with Platonic Theism, the Patristics and Medieval Scholastics developed a different Platonic theory that avoided this problem. Abstract entities were located within the mind of God as divine ideas. This theory of the divine ideas is most famous in the writings of Augustine and flourishes in the hands of Aquinas.[10] As divine ideas, abstract entities are every much a part of the divine essence as the divine properties are, and they exist *a se* within the divine essence. As a result, Augustine

---

9 William Lane Craig, *God Over All: Divine Aseity and the Challenge of Platonism* (Oxford University Press, 2017), 43. See also Brian Leftow, "Is God an Abstract Object?" *Nous* 24, no. 4 (1990): 581–598; idem, *God and Necessity* (Oxford University Press, 2012), 234–235.

10 See Augustine, *Eighty-three Questions,* in *The Fathers of the Church,* vol. 70, trans. David Mosher (Catholic University of America Press, 1982), 79–81; see also Augustine's *De Trinitate,* in The Fathers of the Church 18, trans. Stephen McKenna (Catholic University of America Press, 1963), 9.6.9–11, 12.14.22–23, 12.15.24, and *On Free Choice of the Will,* trans. Anna Benjamin and L. H. Hackstaff (Prentice Hall, 1964), 2.13, 2.8; Thomas Aquinas, *Summa Theologica,* trans. Blackfriars (McGraw-Hill Book Company, 1964), 1a.15.1–2, 1a.16.1–2, 1a.16.5, 1a.16.7–8; Thomas Aquinas, *Summa contra Gentiles,* 1.60–62; Thomas Aquinas, *Truth,* vol. 1, trans. Robert Mulligan (Henry Regnery Company, 1952), 1.2, 1.4, 1.7–8, 3.1–2. For other Christian positions on universals, see Nathan A. Jacobs, "On the Metaphysics of God and Creatures in the Eastern Pro-Nicenes," *PT* 28, no. 1 (2016): 3–42; Richard Cross, "Gregory of Nyssa on Universals," *Vigiliae Christianae* 56 (2002): 372–410; Anna Zhyrkova, "John Damascene's Notion of Being: Essence vs. Hypostical Existence," *SVTQ* 54 (2010): 85–105. For contemporary discussions on the theory of the divine ideas, see also Joseph Koterski, *An Introduction to Medieval Philosophy* (Wiley-Blackwell, 2009), 63–64; Frederick Copleston, *A History of Philosophy,* book 1, vol. 2 (Image Books, 1985), 59–60, 154; Mark Jordan, "The Intelligibility of the World and the Divine Ideas in Aquinas," *RM* 38, no. 1 (1984): 17, 19.

calls them eternal, uncreated reasons.[11] These divine ideas are also considered to be exemplars for all aspects of reality and are the formal causes by which God creates.[12] Alvin Plantinga supports that universals are divine ideas by arguing that anti-Platonic philosophers tend to abandon Platonic realism in favor of antirealism because they cannot conceive how truths can be independent of the mind as Platonism claims. Plantinga agrees by stating that Platonism is what he calls realism run amok. He also agrees that such Platonic truths are based in noetic activity, but not human noetic activity. These truths are based in divine noetic activity since the divine ideas are metaphysical forms that define reality. A proposition is true if and only if it is believed by God, and he assents to it. Propositions are not true because God believes them. Rather, God believes these propositions because they are true. As a result, God possesses the property of necessarily thinking the ideas he thinks since the things that he thinks are the ground for truth.[13]

Supporters of created abstract entities are not persuaded by this conceptualist move or the Platonic move. Matthew Davidson sees three motivations a person can have for accepting a theory of created abstract entities rather than uncreated ones. First, Col 1:16–17 states that God is the creator of all things visible and invisible. Unlike the Platonic supporter, Davidson argues that such a passage can be thought to claim that abstract entities fall into this purview of creation even though the biblical authors did not have them specifically in mind. Second, uncreated abstracts entities are a possible challenge to God's self-sufficiency. God does not need to depend on or look outside himself for knowledge and guidance in creation. Third, perfect being theology holds that it is more perfect to have everything that is distinct from oneself also be dependent on oneself.[14]

---

[11] Augustine, *Eighty-three Questions*, 79–81; Koterski, *Introduction*, 67. Augustine notes that *formae* is the Latin translation of the Greek *ideis*. Plato's Forms are literally ideas that properly exist within a mind.

[12] Koterski, *Introduction*, 74. See also Pseudo-Dionysius, *Divine Names*, trans. C. E. Holt (Macmillan Company, 1940), 5.1–10. See Kenny, *God of the Philosophers*, 15–16.

[13] Alvin Plantinga, "How to be an Anti-Realist," *PAAPA* 56, no. 1 (1982): 68–70; idem, "Augustinian Christian Philosophy," *The Monist* 75, no. 3 (1992): 291–320. See also Greg Welty, "Theistic Conceptual Realism: the Case for Interpreting Abstract Objects as Divine Ideas" (D.Phil. thesis, University of Oxford, 2006); idem, "Truth as Divine Ideas: A Theistic Theory of the Property 'Truth'," *SWJT* 47, no. 1 (2004): 55–69; idem, "Theistic Conceptual Realism," in *Beyond the Control of God?: Six Views on the Problem of God and Abstract Entities*, ed. Paul Gould (Bloomsbury, 2014), 81–96.

[14] Matthew Davidson, "A Demonstration against Theistic Activism," *RS* 35 (1999): 278–279. Davidson argues that the creationist must reject a simple logical dependence between God and abstract entities. This dependence implies that abstract entities entail God and vice versa without need for a creation. The creationist must also reject a non-annihilation dependence where an object's continued existence depends on another. Then God can destroy abstract

A further reason for rejecting uncreated abstract entities is that if abstract entities are part of the divine nature, then God's being is dependent on things that have nothing to do with him or his being, like *Socrates is sitting* or *the property of being red*.¹⁵ This consequence seems just as troubling as having God depend on entities that are external to and independent of his being. This criticism is not to say that the concept of divine ideas as abstract entities is completely rejected, for many creationist philosophers have proposed created abstract entities as divine ideas.¹⁶ Instead of being an uncreated part of the divine nature, divine ideas are brought into being either necessarily or contingently via God's creative thinking. Others have completely rejected the existence of abstract entities because of the various issues and concerns presented here.¹⁷

In rejecting Platonic, Conceptualist, and Creationist theories, William Lane Craig argues for three reasons to accept metaphysical nominalism: the rejection of abstract entities particularly universals. First, abstract entities are

---

entities but not create them. Third is the rejection of a conceptual dependence where abstract entities are understood only by first understanding God. This dependence is a semantical or epistemological relationship, and it is false. Causal dependence is all that is left. See ibid., 280–282.

15 This problem can be magnified if one accepts divine simplicity, making such propositions and properties identical to the divine nature. Thus, God is identical with *Socrates is sitting* and *the property of being red*. But how can the divine being be either propositions or properties, particularly ones that neither reference him nor apply to him? It is one thing to say that God is identical to propositions that reference God, who can be their truthmaker, and that God is identical to any possible proposition or property. However, if all propositions and properties are contained within and entailed by one massive proposition, such as *God is divine*, or property, such as *the property of being divine*, then God could be identical to *that* proposition and property without strictly being identical to *all* propositions and properties. See Aquinas, *Theologica*, 1a.15.2; Aquinas, *Truth*, 3.2; Copleston, 359–360; Aaron Martin, "Reckoning with Ross: Possibles, Divine Ideas, and Virtual Practical Knowledge," *PACPA* 78 (2005): 195–198; Nicholas Wolterstorff, *On Universals* (University of Chicago Press, 1970), 286; Alvin Plantinga, *Does God Have a Nature?* (Marquette University Press, 2007); William Vallicella, "Divine Simplicity: A New Defense," *FP* 9, no. 4 (1992): 508–525.

16 See Christopher Menzel, "Theism, Platonism, and the Metaphysics of Mathematics," *FP* 4, no. 4 (1987): 365–382; Scott Davison, "Could Abstract Objects Depend Upon God?" *RS* 27 (1991): 485–497; Michael Bergmann and Jeffery Brower, "A Theistic Argument Against Platonism (and in Support of Truthmakers and Divine Simplicity)," in *Oxford Studies in Metaphysics*, ed. Dean Zimmerman, vol. 2 (University of Oxford Press, 2006), 357–386; Thomas Morris, *Anselmian Explorations* (University of Notre Dame Press, 1987), 161–178; Richard Davis, *The Metaphysics of Theism and Modality* (Peter Land, 2001); Richard Davis, "God and the Platonic Horde: a Defense of Limited Conceptualism," *PC* 13, no. 2 (2011): 289–303; Paul Gould and Richard Davis, "Modified Theistic Activism," in *Beyond the Control of God*, ed. Gould, 51–64.

17 See Leftow, "God and the Problem of Universals," 325–356; Leftow, "Is God an Abstract Object?," 581–598; William Lane Craig, "A Nominalist Perspective on God and Abstract Objects," *PC* 13, no. 2 (2011): 305–318; William Lane Craig, "Nominalism and Divine Aseity," *Oxford Studies in Philosophy of Religion* 4 (2011): 44–65; Paul Copan and William Lane Craig, *Creation Out of Nothing* (Baker Academic, 2004), 167–196.

queer entities that cause all sorts of problems. They are best discarded. Secondly, creation *ex nihilo* seems to presume the creation of all objects, even abstract entities, and thus presumes the truth of nominalism. Third, the biblical witness indicates that God is *a se* and the sole eternal entity. He is the source of all things other than himself.[18] While there is ultimately nothing inherently incompatible with God and the existence of abstract entities, Craig sees no good metaphysical or theological reason to hold to abstract entities. Craig notes a range of anti-realist options the theist might take: fictionalism (where reference to abstract entities is literally false yet useful discourse), figuralism (where discourse on abstract entities is nothing more than figurative language, not literal reference), and pretense theory (where discourse on abstract entities is merely imaginative in order to explain or understand reality).[19] As a result, a theist need not believe in the existence of abstract entities as philosophically and theologically necessary for explaining reality. Instead, as Brian Leftow asserts, all entities are concrete particulars, and God possesses the ultimate scheme of classification for these concrete particulars. He is the ultimate ground for mind-causation of properties (rather than properties causing mental recognition), and he is the ground for applying concepts to objects (rather than objects being the ground for concepts).[20] By removing abstract entities from the equation, one no longer has to contend with their relationship to God or even to reality itself. Thus, abstract entities are not seen as necessary to a proper understanding of God's nature and his omniscience.

Criticism of Created Abstract Entities and Nominalism

What one believes concerning God's relationship with abstract entities will ultimately affect what one believes concerning divine omniscience. What is the source and ground for the truth of the divine knowledge? Is knowledge something that God receives from another source external to his being? Is it grounded in his nature, or is it established by his creative power? While the content of God's knowledge may not be affected, the manner in which

---

18 Craig, "Nominalism and Divine Aseity," 44–65; Craig and Copan, *Creation Out of Nothing*, 173; Craig, "A Nominalist Perspective on God and Abstract Objects," 305–306; idem, "Anti-Platonism," in *Beyond the Control of God*, ed. Gould, 113–115. The argument of queerness goes both ways. All objects can be queer in the hands of a metaphysician. Second, there is no presumption for nominalism, since other theories can accommodate traditional theistic claims. See Gould, "God and Abstract Objects," 271–274.

19 See Craig, *God Over All*, 144–205. Craig specifically applies these theories to mathematics.

20 Leftow, "God and the Problem of Universals," 339–347.

God knows is affected. What then is the correct theory? There are reasons why I believe that theories of created abstract entities are suspect and give credence for thinking that the theory of uncreated divine ideas is the correct theory to follow rather than accepting Platonic Theism or nominalism, which I conclude are theologically unacceptable.

The first major criticism of created abstract entities is the Bootstrapping Problem. As explained, Platonic entities are independent of and uncreated by God and believed to challenge divine sovereignty and aseity. These abstract entities must be based in the being of God to avoid these implications. The advocate of created abstract entities must explain how God can create universals and properties when he needs to have a property of creating properties. Properties are either separate or the constituent parts of an object. They are both logically and explanatorily prior to the object. Properties must precede the object, and the object bears a dependence relation with properties that the property does not bear to the object. Such a relationship is asymmetrical.[21] Gould argues that there are different senses of logical and explanatory priority. First, there is a conceptual definition: that Adam is my brother-in-law is partially explained by Adam being my wife's brother. Second is a metaphysical definition: a human person is explained partially by the property of humanity. Third is a causal definition: the ball flying through the window partially explains the broken window. Gould argues that certain creationist accounts involve two different senses of explanation: causal and metaphysical. God causes the existence of the divine properties and is metaphysically explained by them. If properties are divine ideas, then God must exist prior to them in order to think them; however, the property of creating abstract entities must exist prior to God's thinking it. Such theories of created abstract entities are incoherent.[22]

Another objection for creationist theories is that the divine properties and the divine essence are all created, but these things must be prior to God's creation of abstract entities. As a result, such theories fail. For example, God causes himself both to exist and to be omnipotent. Being omnipotent contains the property *being exemplified by God*. Thus, by creating the property of omnipotence, God also causes the property to be exemplified by himself. God, however, cannot do this because it implies causal circularity. The exemplification of omnipotence must be prior to creating the property of omnip-

---

21 Paul Gould, "Theistic Activism," *PC* 13 (2011): 128–133.
22 Ibid., 136–138. Gould also argues that on this account God creates all other non-essential ideas as well, such as possible worlds and objects. This criticism is directed primarily at Thomas Morris's account of Absolute Creationism, also known as Theistic Activism. See Morris, *Anselmian Explorations*, 161–78.

otence. The same criticism applies to the divine essence. Being God requires the property of *being necessarily exemplified*, so God causes the necessary exemplification of his own being when he creates the property of *being God*. This relation is incoherent. Further, this criticism can be applied to the truth value that propositions possess. God makes them true by making them exemplify being true. This claim can also be extended to possible worlds where God creates all of these abstract entities and truths in every possible world including the actual world.[23] Theories of uncreated abstract entities avoid these problems. By making abstract entities either independent of God or residing within the divine mind, there is no worry about the priority of divine being over the divine properties.[24] Divine properties exist either prior to or *a se* with the divine being; therefore, such theories do not succumb to the Bootstrapping Problem.

This is not to say that theories of created abstract entities do not have ways of countering the bootstrapping concern. There are at least two ways the creationist can counter the bootstrapping worry. First, one can argue that God is an Aristotelian substance who exemplifies his properties in his being rather than them being the exemplification of an abstract entity. These properties are *a se* with the rest of the divine being; therefore, the divine properties are not dependent on anything outside of God. Second, one could reject a constituent ontology where God is constructed of his properties in favor of a relational ontology where God merely has a relationship with certain abstract entities that reflect the nature of his being. This relationship can occur posterior to the creation of abstract entities, and God does not need to depend on abstract entities for his existence.[25] By exempting God's properties from the exemplification requirements of all other properties or rejecting the requirements altogether, a proponent of created abstract entities can counter the bootstrapping worry and continue to challenge the theory of divine ideas.

A second and more troubling criticism is what I term the *Tabula Rasa* Problem. All theories of created abstract entities argue that abstract entities are created by God either as divine ideas or as abstract entities separate from the divine being. Now, if God produces the divine ideas via his creative thinking, then logically prior to that creation God's mind is a *tabula rasa*: a blank slate. Even if these ideas are necessarily created by God, he does not possess any ideas prior to that creative act. If abstract entities are claimed to be created, then the theist must reject any prior knowledge of these entities in God's

---

23 Davidson, "A Demonstration against Theistic Activism," 287–290.
24 Gould, "Theistic Activism," 138–139; Yandell, "God and Propositions," 284.
25 Craig, *God Over All*, 68–71.

mind. As a result, God is not essentially omniscient. He must produce knowledge rather than simply have knowledge. Such an implication is inimical to a proper understanding of God. God's mind is never a *tabula rasa* even from a logical standpoint, so God cannot create his own ideas. If God creates these abstract entities, then such a creation implies the logically prior existence of knowledge of those objects. God cannot create what he does not already know by nature. As a result, abstract entities (i.e. divine ideas) already exist in God's nature prior to their creation by God since God is essentially omniscient. He cannot exist without his ideas, so there is no need for him to create his own ideas. If these abstract entities already exist essentially and *a se* in the divine nature, then God's creative activity is not the true source of origin for abstract entities.

Further, if any abstract entities are created independent of God's being, then it seems that they are the exemplification of the divine ideas since God is essentially omniscient and creates via his knowledge. Thus, it is implied that the divine ideas act as abstract entities rendering the need for abstract entities independent of God moot. If all things come from God's knowledge, then why should a theist appeal to created abstract entities independent of God? The divine ideas are the exemplars of these independent abstract entities. If the divine ideas can do all of the metaphysical heavy lifting of exemplification, then why have a metaphysical redundancy? It seems that proponents of created abstract entities must accept the theory of uncreated abstract entities as divine ideas in order to remain philosophically and theologically coherent.

The *Tabula Rasa* Problem connects to a third problem for theories that involve created abstract entities. This problem is that any theory of created abstract entities must imply a prior modal framework that grounds God's creative abilities and knowledge. According to theories of created abstract entities, God produces the modal framework by creating abstract entities either in his mind or external to his being; however, I have argued in the previous paragraphs that God cannot create such abstract entities without first having knowledge of what it is that he is creating and that they are possible entities. The modal framework and the abstract entities that establish it, therefore, must exist logically prior to any creation (including the creation of abstract entities) and be known by God. Again, abstract entities must exist uncreated and logically prior to themselves bringing theories of created abstract entities into question.

Catholic theologians were aware of this fact. Anselm argues that all things exist in God's thought prior to their existence in reality. Such prior thoughts are necessary for creation. Anselm compares God's creation to the artist who has an idea in his head and creates his masterpiece according to that idea.[26] He concludes that God must be the source of all things. All divine expression is expression in conjunction with his knowledge; therefore, all things are from him and exist through him. Without God, there is nothing.[27] Aquinas echoes this same idea. In order to act and to work, God must possess an idea of what he is going to do. God's idea is the form which other things imitate. This imitation implies intention to imitate and the presence of an end to that intended imitation.[28] All of God's creative activity must follow a prior existing modal plan, and the things he creates exist and operate according to that plan because anything external to God must be caused by him. Such causation requires prior knowledge of what is being caused.[29] From this divine intellect, God understands all things that are possible about reality.[30]

Given this aspect of divine creation, one must conclude that abstract entities and the modal framework exist prior to *any* divine creation. Because abstract entities and modal truths are not part of the divine creation, theories of created abstract entities appear to be false. An implication of these creationist theories is that if God does not create abstract entities, then God is not free to create the framework of reality. Further, God cannot do what is logically impossible. He cannot violate any principle of the modal framework of which he is aware. God is constrained by a logical determination in the things that he is able to create both abstract and non-abstract.[31] God is not an absolutely free being. He must operate within the bounds of an existing modal reality that proceed from his nature rather than his creative will.

Nominalism also appears to be an unacceptable metaphysical framework for God's omniscience. Biblical doctrine appears to require the existence of abstract entities. For example, the doctrine of the *imago dei* states that all human beings are made in God's image. This image is a property of each individual; therefore, this ontological reality is shared among all human beings. Since nominalism rejects any shared properties among objects, then nominalism is incapable of supporting the doctrine of the *imago dei*.[32] A simi-

---

26 Anselm, *St. Anselm: Basic Writings, The Monologion,* trans. S. N. Deane (Open Court Publishing, 1968), IX–X.
27 Ibid., XII–XIV.
28 Aquinas, *Truth,* 3.1.
29 Aquinas, *Gentiles,* 1.51.5.
30 Ibid., 1.55.
31 Davison, "Could Abstract Objects Depend Upon God?," 494–495.
32 Graham Floyd, "*Imago Dei*: Why Christians Should Believe in Abstract Entities," Evangelical Philosophical Society, http://www.epsociety.org/userfiles/Graham%20Floyd-imago%20dei%20note%20final.pdf.

lar argument can be applied to the idea of goodness. God is said to be good, and God proclaims in the first chapter of Genesis that the creation is good. If there are no sharing of properties among objects, then both God and creation cannot be good. Either one, the other, or none are actually good. Such a conclusion also brings into question the truthfulness of Scripture and the claims it makes.

Other problems arise when one looks closely at Craig's proposed anti-realist positions. Consider fictionalism. This position argues that universals, abstract entities, and properties are mere fictions that do not correspond to any reality. They are merely linguistic functions that are useful for predication. They are realistically false but conventionally true according to the standard linguistic accounts in which they fit.[33] Under fictionalism, the divine concepts would simply be useful fictions that God utilizes to represent and refer to reality. Fictionalism seems to imply that the divine knowledge of reality is not ultimate truth but mere fiction God dreamt up. How then does God possess knowledge if what he knows is merely fiction to him instead of based on a reality? How can it be said that God is omnipotent if the objects he can possibly create are fictitious to him in the way that Middle Earth is fictitious to J. R. R. Tolkien? Tolkien can dream of Middle Earth, but he cannot make it exist. God is supposed to be able to do both. If the concept of a human being or the divine image is just a dreamt fiction to God, then how can he make such things actual objects?[34]

The same implication applies to positions like figuralism and pretense theory. For figuralism, abstract entities are not real but merely figures of speech used to convey some truth, and pretense theory argues that abstract entities are merely imaginations like hypothetical situations used to under-

---

[33] Craig and Copan, *Creation Out of Nothing*, 180–183, 193–195. Craig argues that God may have employed such useful fictions to create the world. It could be argued that God exists as a concrete particular and then forms the concept of omnipotence by examining himself logically posterior to his existence.

[34] This argument can be applied further to the biblical revelation. If God's concepts are fictions and not based on any reality, then is the biblical revelation true, inerrant, and interpretable? When God or the Bible states that "God is holy" or "murder is wrong," terms such as "holy" and "wrong" can be nothing more than useful fictions, not real objects to which one may refer. What then is holiness and wrongness? Do such terms have any real implications for reality? If these concepts are based in fiction, then the above claims appear to be false for they do not correspond to any reality. Thus, God and the Scripture are false since wrongness and holiness do not really exist, and hermeneutics will be much more difficult without knowing whether a claim refers to something real. For more on these issues, see R. Scott Smith, "Craig, Anti-Platonism, and Objective Morality," PC 19, no. 2 (2017): 331–343; idem, "William Lane Craig's Nominalism, Essences, and Implications for Our Knowledge of Reality," PC 15, no. 2 (2013): 365–382; idem, "Craig's Nominalism and the High Cost of Preserving Divine Aseity," EJPR 9, no. 1 (2017): 87–107.

stand reality but which have no reality themselves. Like fictionalism, it is not apparent how such theories are compatible with an all-knowing and creative God. If what God knows is merely figurative or imaginative, then on what metaphysical grounds can God make these things actual? Does God even possess knowledge of reality if his knowledge does not even represent or reflect reality? These theories have even further troubling concerns. Given the implications of these anti-realist theories, both God and the biblical witness appear to be literally stating falsehoods in their claims. When the Bible says that all human beings are created in God's image, this claim must be literally false since the *imago dei* is just a concept that has no reality. When God says that creation is "good," his claim must literally be false since there is no entity called *goodness* that can be exemplified among multiple objects. Such implications as these are inimical to a proper understanding of God and the biblical witness leaving nominalism theologically and philosophically unsuitable as a metaphysical ground for God's omniscience.

Finally, these nominalist theories only work if there is a modal framework already in place such that God can create these fictional ideas, use this figurative language, or develop hypothetical situations. Without a modal framework in place prior to God's creation of these things to establish their possibility, it would be logically impossible for God to think these things. This modal framework, however, would need to be based in the mind of God or exist separate and abstract from the divine being. As a result, the only way Craig's nominalist position can work is if a theory of abstract entities is true, rendering nominalism incoherent. Nominalism rejects what it needs to be true.

Assessment

As this section has argued, it seems that God does not create abstract entities (i.e. universals). Such entities must exist apart from the divine creation for there to be a divine creation. The theory of divine ideas is superior to Platonic Theism since it removes the worry concerning the possibility that God would be dependent on abstract entities. Under the theory of divine ideas, abstract entities and modal truths exist uncreated within the mind of God and *a se* within the divine nature. As a result, God does not need to create his nature for it exists *a se* with the divine ideas. God is not ignorant because he knows all possible things in the divine ideas. No prior modal framework is needed, for God's knowledge is the modal framework of reality. Further, nominalism appears to be antithetical to orthodox theology given its implications regarding God's knowledge of and ability to create reality. Since such theories are suspect and Platonic Theism brings up troubling concerns, I adopt the theory of divine ideas as the metaphysical basis for reality and the grounds for God's knowledge of all possibility. God is omniscient because it is part of his nature to possess all knowledge of what is possible as well as what is actual and to use that knowledge to establish reality.

Defining Omniscience

Having established God's relationship to abstract entities and truth, this study can proceed to developing an understanding of the property of omniscience and tackle the central problem of foreknowledge and divine freedom. This section examines the notion of omniscience in conjunction with the theory of divine ideas as the proper understanding of the property of divine omniscience. Major aspects of omniscience are taken into account when dealing with the notion of the compatibility of divine freedom and omniscience. The most important implication addressed is the implication that God is able to know the future via the divine ideas.

Essential Property

First, omniscience is an essential property of the divine nature and thus a great-making aspect of the divine being. Omniscience is a necessary condition for divinity and a necessary property of divinity.[35] Any being who is not omniscient is not God. This implication also fits well with perfect being theology. Given perfect being theology, God must have complete knowledge because such knowledge is intrinsically good and great-making.[36] Since God is the highest and most perfect of all beings, naturally he must possess complete knowledge of all reality, possible and actual, within his perfect being. God's knowledge should be full and complete, including every truth and fact with nothing left out.[37]

Further, a being with greater cognitive powers than God is impossible. Since God is the highest, most perfect being, God must have unsurpassable cognitive power. Charles Taliaferro illustrates this argument with the follow-

---

35 Thomas Morris, *Our Idea of God* (University of Notre Dame Press, 1991), 88–89. Aquinas also emphasizes that knowledge is an essential aspect of God's nature; though he does so in terms of his view of divine simplicity. See Aquinas, *Summa Theologica*, 1a.14.2; 1a.16.5; idem, *Truth*, 2.3; idem, *Summa contra Gentiles*, 1.45.1–5; 1.46.1–6; 1.47–48.

36 Morris, *Idea*, 83–84; Katherine Rogers, *Perfect Being Theology* (Edinburgh University Press, 2000), 71.

37 George Mavrodes, "Omniscience," in *A Companion to Philosophy of Religion*, ed. Philip Quinn and Charles Taliaferro (Blackwell Publishers, 1997), 236.

ing example. Christopher knows all truths directly and immediately without the need of any intermediary to provide him those truths, but Dennis knows all truths because Christopher informs him. Christopher has a higher cognitive power than Dennis even though Dennis knows all truths. Both can be said to be omniscient, so simple definitions of omniscience (that a person knows all truths) are insufficient due to the difference in the mode of knowing.[38] Knowledge implies power, particularly cognitive power, and there are different degrees of power. Not only God's possession of knowledge but also how he knows is what makes him cognitively excellent.[39] Jonathan Kvanvig also heralds this claim. Cognitive perfection involves three aspects: essential omniscience, maximal and perfect cognitive powers, and a relation between these two such that anything that such a being knows is a result of employing those powers. Kvanvig goes on to state that if all things depend upon God, propositions which God cannot grasp are impossible.[40] Since such a conclusion is impossible, God must know all propositions essentially and perfectly. This understanding of the great-making aspect of omniscience leads to the conclusion that God's knowledge is direct. He does not depend on any intermediary to deliver knowledge to him in an indirect manner.[41] This conclusion fits with the theory of divine ideas and seems incompatible with Platonic Theism.

What is meant by direct perception of truths? William Alston notes that human beings cannot comprehend all facts together. People cannot grasp the particular as a whole. Instead, they must separate facts to relate them logically. God does not have to carve up his knowledge in this way. Alston proposes that since beliefs are propositional attitudes carved up, God does not have beliefs.[42] Now, one could argue that whatever qualification is attached to true belief does not apply to God, such as justification, warrant, reliable formation, epistemic obligations, etc. Alston, however, does not believe that this solution is promising. Instead, Alston argues for intuitive knowledge which is when some fact is immediately-directly present to the mind without need of an intermediary. Thus, intuitive knowledge is not like a proposition which can be believed without direct presentation. Intuitive knowledge requires the

---

38 Charles Taliaferro, "Divine Cognitive Power," *IJPR* 18 (1985): 133–134; idem, "Unknowable Truths and Omniscience: A Reply to Kvanvig," *JAAR* 61 (1993): 554–556.

39 Taliaferro, "Divine Cognitive Power," 135–136. See also Anselm, *Proslogion*, VI.

40 Jonathan Kvanvig, "Unknowable Truths and the Doctrine of Omniscience," *JAAR* 57 (1989): 490, 496. Taliaferro disputes this claim saying that the logically impossible and the future are possible unknowable truths. See Taliaferro, "Unknowable," 558–561.

41 Morris, *Idea*, 84.

42 William Alston, "Does God Have Beliefs?" in *Divine Nature and Human Language* (Cornell University Press, 1989), 183.

mental state of immediate presence of the fact to the consciousness. One, therefore, can have a belief without it being the case, but one cannot have knowledge without it being the case.[43] Since God is most perfect in all ways, he will possess this most ideal state of knowledge because God never needs to assent to a belief if he is immediately aware. Beliefs are not necessary for action since intuitive knowledge can fill the gap.[44]

William Hasker, however, is not convinced by Alston's claims. He asks what exactly it is of which an intuitive knower is aware. What is directly present to the knower? Is it some sort of internal representation that is guaranteed to be adequate and correct? Possibly, but Hasker claims Alston does not defend this view. Instead, Hasker notes that according to Alston what God knows is the actual fact and not some divine representation.[45] Hasker argues that this intuitive knowledge is incoherent when combined with the concept of timeless eternity. Physical facts are in time and experience change. How can such things be viewed intuitively in timelessness? What temporal moment of a physical fact does God intuitively know? God knows them all. All temporal moments of a physical fact must be simultaneous, which means that the physical fact is really timeless, not temporal.[46]

Given this argument from timeless eternity, Hasker states that an eternal God must be intuitively aware by an inner representation; however, Hasker thinks it better to know physical facts directly rather than by some similitude in the divine mind. God, therefore, must be temporal. Yet, the only time that God can be directly aware of is the present. To be aware of any other time God must have inner representations of this reality. Such an inner representation, however, conforms to Alston's definition of a belief as a state that is just what it is regardless of any fact. If such a representation is taken as being true, then it is a belief. Knowledge, therefore, about times other than the present must be beliefs. These representations do not need to be propositional. Rather, they may be similar to a working model, like a graphical image, that contains all the information that needs to be known without being splintered into varying propositions. Hasker calls this an inner model of the entire system that does not require a propositional representation.[47]

The theory of divine ideas shows Hasker's argument to be incorrect. According to the theory of divine ideas, God's ideas are not a representation of the physical fact; rather, they are abstract entities of which God is directly

---

43 Ibid., 185–187.
44 Ibid., 190–192.
45 William Hasker, "Yes, God has Beliefs!" *RS* 24 (1988): 387–388.
46 Ibid., 389.
47 Ibid., 389–393.

aware. As universals and exemplars, the divine ideas are truths about reality, not mere representations. Physical reality is the representation. Since they are not mediated to God, then God knows them by an absolute and immediate direct awareness. Thus, one need not assert that the divine ideas are representations. They are truths that can be known timelessly and directly without representation; therefore, they are not beliefs. Thus, Hasker's claims fail. On the other hand, God's direct awareness of his ideas does not mean that he does not also have an absolute and immediate direct awareness of physical reality as well. Nothing in the theory of divine ideas states that God knows physical reality via his ideas. Knowledge of abstract reality and its modal truths is different from knowledge of physical reality and its actual facts. God may be directly aware of his idea of Smith while also being directly aware of Smith in his physical existence. As a result, God has an absolute and immediate direct awareness of all things in his mind and in physical reality, and this awareness need not be propositional in nature nor require temporal existence.

How then should God's knowledge be viewed? Traditionally, God has been thought to possess all propositional knowledge and to be perfectly acquainted with all things. This claim is expressed as both *de dicto* and *de re* knowledge.[48] Is this view correct? Propositions are typically thought to be real, abstract objects that are the foundations of sentences and claims, but God does not create according to these propositions like some Platonic demiurge. He sees and sustains all things in his vision. Thus, God does not know *by* propositions since that would be indirect knowledge rather than direct knowledge. Such propositionally structured knowledge is inappropriate for God because it is splintered.[49] In support of the non-propositional view, Aquinas states that God knows *of* propositions because he knows human beings who know propositions. He knows them not by putting them together or by knowing the terms, but he knows their essence by his simple knowledge of divine ideas.[50] Stephen Davis states that one cannot define omniscience as knowledge of *all* propositions. There are false propositions that cannot be known because

---

48 Morris, *Idea*, 86–87.
49 Rogers, *Perfect Being*, 76–77; Zagzebski, "Omniscience," in *The Routledge Companion to Philosophy of Religion*, ed. Chad Meister and Paul Copan (Routledge, 2007), 263. The possession of propositional beliefs by God is not necessarily incompatible with a proper understanding of God. God's nature could provide him with propositionally structured divine ideas along with eternal direct awareness of both those propositions and physical facts. Further, God's propositional beliefs would be the metaphysical grounds for all human propositional belief. Also, these propositional beliefs need not be carved up if they are all contained in one massive proposition: namely, the proposition about God and his nature.
50 Aquinas, *Summa Theologica*, 1a.14.14.

they are illogical, like 2+2=5. Also, omniscience cannot be defined as knowing any true proposition for such a definition does not exclude the possibility of inconsistently believing false ones as well.[51]

Further, a number of difficulties arise concerning God's knowledge of propositions. Edward Wierenga excellently condenses these arguments. First, he considers the *de re* arguments against omniscience. Having first been put forward by A. N. Prior, the *de re* argument claims that there is a species of beliefs about objects and the properties they possess. Ralph might know the provost of his college and the type of person the provost is. Ralph, however, could fail to recognize the provost in a dark alley and think him suspicious without knowing that *of* the provost. Ralph does not believe that the provost is suspicious and therefore does not know that the provost is suspicious since he has failed to associate the provost with the dark figure in the alley. Some philosophers argue in response that *de re* beliefs require one to be in some relation of acquaintance with the object: to be in rapport with it. This rapport could be achieved by an appropriate concept, the object itself, or a right causal relation to it. Thus, *de re* knowledge is only a species of *de dicto* knowledge. This conclusion does not mean that God is causally impinged upon by an object. It only means that God must sustain some relation that is sufficient to give him *de re* knowledge. Wierenga claims that the notions of God creating, sustaining, and being in direct awareness of all things is a sufficient relation to turn *de re* beliefs into *de dicto* ones. If *de re* belief is not reducible to *de dicto* ones, then one can add a clause to his (D1) definition of omniscience to get the proper definition:

(D1) S is omniscient=df. for every proposition p, if p is true, then S knows p, and for any x and property P, if x has P, then S knows of x that x has P.[52]

Since God knows and is directly aware of all things both in the divine mind and in physical reality, God does possess a relationship with the objects in question such that he knows them *de re* and knows them infallibly. He could convert this knowledge into *de dicto* knowledge, but he does not need to do so.

---

51 Stephen Davis, *Logic and the Nature of God* (Eerdmans, 1983), 26.
52 Edward Wierenga, "Omniscience," in *The Oxford Handbook of Philosophical Theology*, ed. Thomas Flint and Michael Rea (Oxford University Press, 2009), 134. For an analysis of these criticisms against God's knowledge of *de re* propositions, see A. N. Prior, "Formalities of Omniscience," in *Papers on Time and Tense* (Oxford University Press, 2003), 39–59; Roderick Chisholm, "Knowledge and Belief: *de dicto* and *de re*," PS 29 (1976): 1–20; David Lewis, "Attitudes *de dicto* and *de se*," PR 88 (1979): 513–543; David Kaplan, "Quantifying In," *Synthese* 29 (1968): 178–214.

Wierenga notes that Norman Kretzmann argues that omniscience cannot include knowledge of propositions that include temporal or *de se* indexicals, at least in compatibility with timelessness and immutability. How can a timeless God know facts and truths couched in personal and temporal terms? Nicholas Wolterstorff and Stephen Davis have argued against the notion of divine timelessness along these lines.[53] In response, Kvanvig has argued that these types of propositions only involve a special kind of access or grasping of ordinary propositions. If so, then *de praesenti* and *de se* propositions are reducible to *de dicto* propositions. Wierenga has also argued that such propositions only refer to the haecceity of the person or state of affairs included in the proposition. Nothing prevents God from knowing the haecceity of other people, objects, and times. Also, this distinction between propositions may simply be different perspectives of the same propositional claim. One can believe a proposition is true at an index, and one can believe at an index that a proposition is true. The former can be believed by anyone. The latter can only be known at the specific index in question. Wierenga argues that given this view, *de praesenti* and *de se* propositions are not possible for God to know since they are known at a specific index. Since they are impossible for God to know and no one can do what is impossible, such a lack of knowledge cannot be held against him.[54] Using the theory of divine ideas, it can be argued that God knows the haecceity, or essence, of all people, places, and times in such a way that he grasps the same truths in a different manner than humans do. Thus, Kvanvig and Wierenga's arguments are correct. Also, Thomas Sullivan asserts that this non-propositional knowing demonstrates that something is wrong with the challenge to state what God knows in propositional format. If Sullivan's contention is true, then arguments from indexicals and *de se* knowledge against omniscience are invalid. God could know indexical propositions in a non-propositional way.[55] This conclusion is precisely the case given the theory of divine ideas.

---

53 See Norman Kretzmann, "Omniscience and Immutability," *JP* 63 (1966): 409–421; Nicholas Wolterstorff, "God Everlasting," in *God and the Good*, ed. C. Orlebeke and L. Smeades (Eerdmans, 1975), 181–203; Stephen Davis, *Logic and the Nature of God*, 26–32; A. N. Prior "Formalities of Omniscience"; Kenny, *God of the Philosophers*, 27–50; Patrick Grim, "Against Omniscience: the Case from Essential Indexicals," *Nous* 19 (1985): 151–180.

54 Kvanvig, *Possibility*, 48–50; Wierenga, "Omniscience," 135–137; idem, *The Nature of God*, 46–59; idem, "Timelessness Out of Mind," in *God and Time: Essays on the Divine Nature*, ed. Gregory Ganssle and D. Woodruff (Oxford University Press, 2002), 153–164; E. Sosa, "Consciousness of the Self and of the Present," in *Agent, Language, and the Structure of the World*, ed. J. Tomberlin (Hackett, 1983), 131–147; see also Rogers, *Perfect Being*, 88–89; Mavrodes, "Omniscience," 236–238.

55 Thomas Sullivan, "Omniscience, Immutability, and Divine Knowledge," *FP* 8 (1991): 26, 30–31. It is still too quick to exclude the possibility that God does not know via propositions.

Scope

What then is a proper definition of the property of omniscience? Kvanvig provides the following definition of the concept of omniscience for consideration.

> O: A being B is omniscient=df. B justifiably believes that p iff p is true.

As Kvanvig's definition points out, God must have not only a justification for what he knows but also right reasons for knowing it if he is to be considered an omniscient being. Kvanvig asserts that this understanding can also be couched in terms of essential omniscience.

> EO: Being B is essentially omniscient=df. B has the essential property of justifiably believing that p iff p is true.

Kvanvig goes on to argue that O is immune to Gettier problems that claim that a person can justifiably believe something but on incorrect grounds. These problems assume certain limitations on the knower, but God's omniscience could never have such limitations. God could never hold justified knowledge on non-justifiable grounds.[56] Edward Wierenga also offers a series of definitions for the property of omniscience.

> (D1) S is omniscient=df. for every proposition p, if p is true, then S knows p.

> (D2) S is omniscient=df. for every proposition p, if p is true, then S knows p, and if p is false, then S does not believe p.

> (D3) S is omniscient=df. for every proposition p, either S knows that p is true or S knows that p is false.

First, if all propositional knowledge is reducible to *de dicto* propositions, then both the *de re* and the indexical problem against omniscience are no worry. God knows these propositions in the *de dicto* manner. Second, if all propositional knowledge is reducible to a singular divine *de re* proposition about God, then there is no worry about God's rapport with objects and indexicals. God has a rapport with these objects and indexicals by knowing himself.

56 Jonathan Kvanvig, *The Possibility of an All-Knowing God* (St. Martin's Press, 1986), 33, 35–36. For an explanation of how a person can hold a justified belief on non-justified grounds, see Edmund Gettier, "Is Justified True Belief Knowledge?" *Analysis* 23 (1963): 121–23. Since God is omniscient, he would always be aware of the proper justification for his knowledge.

Wierenga believes that all these definitions are equivalent. It is implausible to think that a being knows something while believing it to be false. If one knows all truths, then one will also know all falsehoods while not assenting to these falsehoods. As a result, God is an infallible knower.[57] These definitions also give rise to a pertinent issue. Both Kvanvig's and Wierenga's proposals define divine knowledge in terms of belief and propositional structure. As was previously argued, God's knowledge is not propositionally structured, and God does not have beliefs. Given the non-propositional viewpoint, I suggest that Kvanvig's definitions be revised using the term "knows" instead of "believes" and "knowing" instead of "believing" so as to explicitly assert a non-propositional viewpoint.

Unchangeable

Omniscience in conjunction with the theory of divine ideas also implies that God's state of knowledge need not experience change; but, what exactly does one mean by change? Aquinas argues for no change of any kind in the state of divine knowledge.[58] Aquinas argues that because of this unchangeableness, God's knowledge is not discursive in nature. God does not need to derive one thing from another or construct concepts because God knows all things completely and directly both in the divine ideas and in physical reality. Since God does not need to derive knowledge of one thing from another, God is not ignorant of things as discursiveness implies. God knows all causes, and he sees all effects in their causes.[59] As a result, God does not need to derive knowledge of some things from his knowledge of other things.

God's knowledge also need not change if he possesses a timeless, direct awareness of all facts, physical and non-physical. God's knowledge would be eternally complete and need not experience temporal change. God's knowledge, therefore, would not be by temporal addition as with human knowledge. God would not know by temporal progression but rather would be fully aware of all things as a whole. Thus, forms and essences flow into things from God's knowledge while human knowledge is the impression of things on the

---

57 Edward Wierenga, "Omniscience," in *The Oxford Handbook of Philosophical Theology*, ed. Thomas Flint and Michael Rea (Oxford University Press, 2009), 130. For more on the notion of infallibility, see Aquinas, *Truth*, 1.10; Alvin Plantinga, "Reason and Belief in God," in *Faith and Reason*, ed. Alvin Plantinga and Nicholas Wolterstorff (University of Notre Dame Press, 1983), 58; Wierenga, "Omniscience," 131–132; Linda Zagzebski, "Omniscience, Time, and Freedom," in *The Blackwell Guide to Philosophy of Religion*, ed. William Mann (Blackwell Publishing, 2005), 5–6; Kvanvig, *Possibility*, 30–32.

58 Aquinas, *Summa Theologica*, 1a.14.15.

59 Ibid., 1a.14.7.

human mind. God always knows all things since he is the action of knowing, not a habit of knowing.[60]

Aquinas sees change and discursiveness as a deficiency since one must know through something else rather than simply knowing. Aquinas believes that God does not know through something else. This retort does not mean that God does not know logical arguments, which are presumably pieced together. Instead, God possesses knowledge *of* all logical arguments, but his knowledge does not *proceed* from such logic. That is, God possesses all logical arguments already worked out rather than having to piece them together. He sees the argument all at once rather than piecemeal. Since God knows by knowing his ideas and by being aware of physical reality, he does not know by composing or deriving. According to Aquinas, a discursive intellect does not consider all things at once as God does.[61] Since divine knowledge is partly composed of the divine ideas and those ideas exist *a se*, then God possesses the ideas all at once without having to learn, derive, or remember them. Wierenga calls this type of possessed knowledge occurrent knowledge. Occurrent knowledge is when a being currently has a proposition or idea in mind. The opposite—dispositional knowledge—is when a being does not currently have a proposition or idea in mind but is disposed to having it in mind. Wierenga notes that according to Aquinas God's knowledge is in no way discursive; therefore, God has occurrent knowledge. He regards all things, physical and non-physical, at once. He does not learn or remember things, so he is not disposed to having a proposition or idea in mind. God also does not logically deduce. Since God is always omniscient and deduction implies learning, God cannot deduce.[62]

One philosopher disputes this conclusion. George Mavrodes thinks that God can know everything by inference. He expresses his view in the following proposition:

(T) For every proposition that God knows, He knows that proposition by inferring it from one or more other propositions that He knows.[63]

Mavrodes first appeals to the existence of an infinite chain of propositions possessed only by an infinite knower to reject foundationalism: that knowl-

---

60 Aquinas, *Truth*, 2.1.
61 Aquinas, *Summa contra Gentiles*, 1.57.9–11, 1.58.1–3.
62 Wierenga, *Nature of God*, 36–38; idem, "Omniscience," 131–132. Alternatively, it might be said that God does not need to deduce rather than that he cannot deduce.
63 George Mavrodes, "How Does God Know the Things He Knows?" in *Divine and Human Action*, ed. Thomas Morris (Cornell University Press, 1988), 345–347.

edge must begin with someone or many non-inferential proposition(s). This infinite chain is both inferential and non-circular and therefore does not fit with coherentism. Mavrodes uses the idea of the infinite set of integers or the continuous addition of propositions together to illustrate this claim.[64] Thus, God's knowledge is bound together by an infinitely long and possibly non-temporal string of inference relations.

Mavrodes goes on to argue that Aquinas believes in both temporal discursiveness (passing from one piece of knowledge to the other) and logical discursiveness (inference). The second is supposed to presuppose the first: one cannot think about both p and q at the same time. Mavrodes, however, rejects this supposition. He says that it actually seems quite possible that they stand alone. He argues that these types of discursiveness have an asymmetrical causal relation that can be viewed together at once without the idea of proceeding from one to the other, but the relation is still logically discursive.[65] If this claim is true, God views the entire inferential chain at once rather than piecing it together discursively. This divine viewpoint is no different from the occurrent view of divine knowledge. The divine ideas, however, are immediately possessed by God as an *a se* part of his nature; therefore, they need not be inferentially composed. An inferential chain of discursive ideas is unnecessary as the basis of the divine knowledge. Mavrodes's claim, however, that foundationalism fails may be incorrect because the divine ideas could fulfill the description of basic, non-inferential propositions or ideas which the theory of foundationalism requires. Mavrodes also objects to the idea that God must know directly. He argues that Aquinas accepts indirect divine knowledge in that God knows things by knowing himself, which is indirect.[66] This argument, however, is unnecessary. God can be directly aware of physical and non-physical reality without the need to know through himself. Thus, Mavrodes's arguments do not demonstrate that the divine omniscience is discursive or that God's knowledge is indirect.[67]

---

64 Ibid., 350–352.
65 Ibid., 355–357. If the chain of inference can be viewed all at once, then God need not be a temporal being.
66 Ibid., 360.
67 One could argue that portions of the divine knowledge are discursive and indirect on the grounds that they are derived from the divine choice. Logically or temporally prior to the divine choice, God is not aware of his choice and its effects since he has not made a choice. Logically or temporally posterior to the divine choice, he is aware of what his choice is and its effects. Thus, one may contend that God discursively and indirectly knows certain things based on the divine choice. These implications, however, do not follow. If God essentially acts and is eternally aware of his acting, then that eternal awareness of the divine acting is direct. Further, the effects of that action are directly perceived. Therefore, it remains questionable that portions of God's knowledge are discursive and indirectly derived from God's act of will.

Creative and Modal

God is also the cause of all things in conjunction with his knowledge. God's knowledge of things stands to those objects as an artist's ideas stand to his creation. God knows, or knows properly, and causes things as a maker knows and causes what he makes; therefore, God creates according to what he knows as possible via the divine ideas. God's existence involves his act of knowing all truths both physical and non-physical; thus, his will is in conjunction with his knowledge. This knowing is a logical consequence rather than a logical production.[68]

As Katherine Rogers states, human beings sense things and abstract the forms of what they sense. This form is the intelligible species which allows people to understand objects. The form is not just a mental object people cogitate on; otherwise, they would have mere opinions. Rather, people understand the object through its intelligible species. God, however, brings things into being via their intelligible species that are in his mind.[69] Thus, God is the cause of all things in conjunction with his ideas.

Because of omniscience and its conjunction with the theory of divine ideas, God knows all actual and possible objects of creation perfectly. God, in knowing essences and natures, knows both the singular and the many, the multitude and the particular, the universal and the distinct. One cannot be known without the other.[70] God knows particulars and individuals because all perfections and properties of particulars and individuals are first found in God's intellect and then expressed in the physical world. God is the cause of things in conjunction with his knowledge. Since God's power extends to both form and matter, his knowledge must include generalities and individualities. He is the artist of both the form and the matter of an object.[71]

God also knows non-actual things because they exist as potential creations in his intellect. God, who views all of time, does not know non-existent things by knowledge of vision but by his simple understanding. As a result, God knows all truths of potentiality in the divine ideas for they are the source of such potentiality.[72] God knows non-existent things as an artist knows things he does not make. The antecedent always exists before the subsequent just as the theoretical exists before the practical. These non-ex-

---

68 Aquinas, *Summa Theologica*, 1a.14.8; *Summa contra Gentiles*, 1.50.3.
69 Rogers, *Perfect Being*, 74–75.
70 Aquinas, *Summa contra Gentiles*, 1.50.6.
71 Aquinas, *Summa Theologica*, 1a.14.11; *Truth*, 2.3–5.
72 Aquinas, *Summa Theologica*, 1a.14.9.

istent things exist as divine ideas even if God does not actualize them.[73] God even knows evil by knowing all goods and the possible corruptions of those goods.[74] Thus, God's omniscient knowledge extends to both actual and possible objects. It is the divine ideas that provide God knowledge of possible objects, and God views all actual objects he creates.

The Future

Since God can know objects in their contingency and can see the history of all possible worlds in the divine ideas, then God can know the future. Aquinas states that contingent events can be known in two ways. They can be known because the events are actual and are viewed as actual, or they can be known as they exist in their causes as possible effects. Aquinas claims that God has the luxury of knowing both; however, the former depends on God being timeless. God would not know contingents successively but as eternally present to his viewpoint: a simultaneous, occurrent whole.[75] This claim is true because God knows causes (forms and essences) and all their effects if they are actualized as well as by their being in eternity within his mind. This knowledge also allows God to know the will and mind of men by knowing their essences (causes) through the divine ideas.[76]

On the other hand, Joshua Hoffman and Gary Rosenkrantz argue that an omniscient being could know the future only if the future could be logically deduced by the divine being. Unfortunately, the future cannot be deduced from any present laws or conditions; therefore, it is not possible to know the future.[77] Given the theory of divine ideas, this claim fails for four reasons. First, all possible worlds are known by God in the divine ideas, which are the source of their essences. God then can know the future outcome of all possible states of reality by these ideas. Second, with these and all other essences located in the divine ideas, causal laws imbedded within these essences can allow for the future to be deduced. This deduction could be directly evident to the divine mind rather than composed. Third, God could know the future by his choice of a possible world to instantiate. If God is aware of the effects that his creative choice will instantiate via the divine ideas, then he can know the future. Fourth, the future can be known if it is actually occurring and God is viewing

---

73 Aquinas, *Truth*, 2.8.
74 Aquinas, *Summa Theologica*, 1a.14.10.
75 Ibid., 1a.14.13; Aquinas, *Truth*, 2.12.
76 Aquinas, *Summa contra Gentiles*, 1.67.1–11; 1.68.1–8.
77 Joshua Hoffman and Gary Rosenkrantz, *The Divine Attributes* (Blackwell Publishing, 2002), 119.

it as it occurs. This latter view assumes the truth of divine timelessness. Thus, Hoffman and Rosenkrantz are incorrect in their claim that the future cannot be known. The future can be known by God. Further, such a possibility follows from the theory of divine ideas. Since possible worlds exist as forms and essences within the divine mind, God is aware of the future of every possible world. He is aware of these futures logically or temporally prior to creating any world, and he is aware of the actual future logically or temporally posterior to creating a certain world. This knowledge of the future encompasses all events and action that occur within the temporal world including divine actions, such as parting the Red Sea. Thus, it appears that God is aware not only of future human actions but is also aware of future divine actions as well.

Conclusion

This chapter explains the concept of omniscience by looking at God's relationship to abstract entities (i.e. universals) and how that relationship ultimately affects the notion of God's knowledge. Theories of created abstract entities and nominalism were rejected on the grounds that they are problematic. Platonic Theism was also rejected in order to avoid issues regarding God's dependence on entities that exist independent of his being. Abstract entities exist as an uncreated and *a se* part of the divine essence and reside as ideas in the divine mind. These ideas are the metaphysical grounds for reality and provide God with all knowledge. As a result, omniscience is a great-making property such that God is cognitively perfect: he knows all things and in the right way. God's knowledge does not need to be propositionally structured, and such a non-propositional structure is superior since it avoids the problems attributed to propositional knowledge.

Because God possesses knowledge of all physical and non-physical facts, that knowledge is infallible. His knowledge also does not need to be changeable due to its infallible nature as well as on the supposition of God's timeless awareness. Such divine ideas in tandem with the divine will are also the cause of things that actually exist, allowing God knowledge not just of actual objects but also of all possible objects, including worlds. A final implication of the theory of divine ideas is that God knows the future, particularly the future as it is defined within the divine ideas of possible worlds. A result of God's ability to know the future is that God also foreknows all future divine action within the temporal world. This final implication is the most pertinent to the problem of foreknowledge and divine freedom. This study now turns to explain this problem and seek a solution.

Chapter 2

The Problem of Divine Freedom

In the first chapter, I outlined the divine property of omniscience in accordance with the theory of divine ideas. An implication of that definition is that God is able to know the future of the actual world by knowing the divine idea he has of that world. Since the actual world will unfold exactly as the divine idea indicates, then God is able to know all temporal events of the actual world prior to the actual world's existence. This foreknowledge also includes divine actions that are part of the history of the actual world, such as the parting of the Red Sea. This exhaustive knowledge of the future composes the central problem of this study. The problem arising from such an understanding of omniscience is known as the problem of foreknowledge and freedom. If God knows the future, then all future events and actions appear to be determined or fixed. They must take place, but how then can it be that agents are free to choose their actions? Agents do not seem to be able to do otherwise, leading to the question of their moral responsibility for their choices and actions. Philosophical literature is no stranger to this problem; thousands of pages have been dedicated to its explication and resolution.

The problem of foreknowledge and freedom is not limited to human choices and actions. As I contend, the problem also applies to God and his choices. If God exhaustively knows the future as the definition of omniscience states, then he also should know his *own* choices and actions prior to engaging in them. These choices and actions include both his choice of what to create as well as those within and in response to his creation. If God knows his own future choices and actions prior to actualizing them, then he is determined and not a free being it appears. If God lacks knowledge of his own future in order to save his freedom, then the definition of omniscience appears compromised. If God does not know the future, then his knowledge is not complete. I investigate this problem for the remainder of this study. In the first section of this chapter, I define the two main types of freedom that agents can possess. In the second section, I present the problem of foreknowledge and divine freedom by applying two versions of the problem of foreknowledge and human freedom to the divine situation. In section three, I examine the contemporary discussion on the issue of foreknowledge and divine freedom and determine the type of freedom God possesses. In the last section, I set up criteria for helping determine a successful solution to the central problem of this study.

Defining Freedom

Before delving into the problem of foreknowledge and divine freedom, it is necessary to understand the notion of freedom. Philosophers define freedom in different ways. Anthony Kenny notes two main conceptions of what it means to be free. First is freedom of indifference, which approaches freedom via ability and power. Freedom of indifference argues that freedom is primarily the ability and capacity of alternative action, or the freedom to act otherwise in the same circumstances. Since the agent can do otherwise, the agent is not determined to one course of action; therefore, this notion of freedom is incompatible with determinism. The second notion of freedom is freedom of spontaneity. This notion of freedom approaches freedom via desire and wanting. An agent acts freely when he is executing what he desires or wants to do. This type of freedom is incompatible with compulsion since a person would not be doing what he desires and wants. It can be compatible with determinism since it is possible that an agent's desires and wants be determined. As a result, an agent's actions can be determined.[1]

William Mann also notes this distinction in the two conceptions of freedom. He provides the following technical conception of liberty (or freedom) of indifference (LI).

> (LI): agent A is free at time t with respect to situation s if and only if A has it in his power at t to bring it about that s and A has it in his power at t to refrain from bringing it about that s.

---

[1] Anthony Kenny, "Freedom, Spontaneity, and Indifference," in *Essays on Freedom of Action*, ed. Ted Honderich (Routledge and Kegan Paul, 1973), 90.

The Problem of Divine Freedom

Mann states that nothing in the causal history before time t or in the psychological states of the agent A is decisive in determining the agent's action.[2] The agent is indifferent as to which alternative to choose, allowing the agent the ability to choose either alternative without having his power to choose any specific alternative diminished or negated. A diminishment of choice over alternatives results in a loss of freedom.

Mann also provides the following conception of liberty (or freedom) of spontaneity (LS).

(LS): A is free to s if and only if A brings it about at t that s because A wants at t to bring it about that s or A refrains from bringing it about at t that s because A wants at t to refrain from bringing it about that s.

Mann states that liberty of spontaneity shows that an agent's wants are causes of actions and that an agent's wants can be caused. Freedom is merely harmony between one's wants and actions. A deterministic causal history or psychological state can be accepted in tandem with liberty of spontaneity as long as an agent's wants are the vehicle for actions.[3] The agent then is free since his action arose from a natural inclination, attitude, or behavior. The agent is not indifferent towards his alternatives because his causal history or natural inclination directs him to desire one alternative over another. Even though the agent's power over certain alternatives is diminished or negated due to this causal history or natural inclination, the agent is still considered to be free since he does what he desires.

These two conceptions of freedom provide the grounds for the two main definitions of freedom used in this study. The libertarian definition of freedom insists upon the concept of liberty of indifference. It stresses the agent's power and ability to choose among possible alternatives. In order to be free, an agent must be able to choose to act or refrain from acting in any situation. No natural, causal, or logical implication should prevent the agent from choosing and acting a certain way. If the agent is not able to enact more than one option in a situation, then the agent is not free and not responsible for his action. On the other hand, the compatibilist definition of freedom advocates the concept of liberty of spontaneity. In order to be free, an agent need only act upon his desires and wants without being coerced or prevented from fulfilling them. According to liberty of spontaneity, an agent's desires and wants

---

2 William Mann, "God's Freedom, Human Freedom, and God's Responsibility for Sin," in *Divine and Human Action*, ed. Thomas Morris (Cornell University Press, 1988), 183–184.

3 Ibid., 184–185.

may be determined. As a result, the agent's actions can be determined; therefore, compatibilist freedom is compatible with determinism, hence its name. I utilize libertarian freedom and compatibilist freedom for the rest of this study for understanding the concept of freedom.

The Problem

Now that the concept of freedom has been defined, I turn to an explication of the problem of foreknowledge and divine freedom. This section proceeds by examining versions of this problem as it pertains to human freedom. I then apply these versions of the problem to the divine situation to show how divine freedom also is endangered by the problem of foreknowledge and freedom.

Pike's Argument

Nelson Pike proposes the first version of the problem of foreknowledge and human freedom to be discussed. In accordance with the definition of omniscience presented in this study, Pike claims that God is an omniscient being and cannot have false beliefs. God knows everything, even the future. Pike also explicitly avoids the timeless understanding of God. Instead, he argues that God exists at all moments of time and holds his knowledge of the past, the present, and the future ever before his mind in an occurrent manner.[4] Pike then offers the following thought experiment. Jones mowed his lawn last Saturday afternoon. Assuming God exists and is (essentially) omniscient, Pike claims that eighty years prior to last Saturday God knew and believed that Jones would mow his lawn at that time. Then Jones was not able (that is it was not within his power) to refrain from that action at that time.[5] If he were, then either God does not know the future or is fallible in his knowledge. Thus, Jones does not seem to be free in respect to mowing his lawn.

Pike claims that if Jones could have refrained from mowing (that is, if Jones possessed the power of refraining from mowing), then Jones would have possessed the power to make it that God held a false belief, which is impossible because of God's infallibility. There are only two other options to escape this problem. First, Jones could have the power to change the past by making it such that eighty years ago God did not hold the belief that he in fact held. Second, Jones could have the power to make it that God did not exist

---

4 Nelson Pike, "Divine Omniscience and Voluntary Action," *PR* 20 (1965): 28–31.
5 Ibid., 31.

eighty years ago. However, no one, not even God, can change the past or make it such that God did not exist at any time.[6] Pike notes that he is not making any claim as to what causes the action; he is arguing that any past belief of God already has a truth claim and cannot be made false.[7] It seems, therefore, that divine foreknowledge negates human freedom.

Pike's argument can also apply to God's acting. At some moment of time, God acted in the world. According to God's knowledge of the future, God believed and knew temporally prior to that moment what he would choose to do. God, therefore, was not able to refrain (did not possess the power to refrain) from choosing and acting in the manner in which he did. If the problem is applied to God's choice of a world to create, the problem is exacerbated. If God knew temporally prior to his creative choice what world he would choose to create, then God was not able to exercise the power to refrain from choosing and creating in the manner that he did. By further application of Pike's argument, God cannot make himself have a false belief, he cannot change his state of belief regarding how he will act, and he cannot make it such that he never existed. Like Jones, God does not seem to be free.

Now, at least two criticisms can be raised against Pike's version of the free will problem. First, William Alston asks what Pike means by "free," "power," "ability," "do otherwise," and "voluntary." He notes that libertarians take such words to mean that one is not causally or logically forced to choose only one option by something that existed in the past, like God's knowledge. Instead, one may choose from many options. The compatibilist, however, argues that a person is free to choose and do *what he chooses*. According to compatibilists, an option being within one's power only requires that a person and his situation be so constituted that his choice to act would obtain. A person could be causally or logically necessitated to choose as he does, but that does not matter. What matters is that the person does what he chooses to do. Alston states that Pike assumes the libertarian understanding of freedom as the only viable understanding of freedom.[8] More will be said on God's type of freedom in proceeding paragraphs.

A second criticism of Pike's version of the free will problem is that he assumes that God is temporal when God could be atemporal. God may not be subject to temporal location and extension. If God is atemporal, what God knew eighty years ago or at any past time is of no concern since there are no

---

6 Ibid., 32–33.
7 Ibid., 35–36.
8 William Alston, "Divine Foreknowledge and Alternative Conceptions of Human Freedom," *IJPR* 18 (1985): 19–32. Pike's argument would be superfluous on the compatibilist understanding of freedom.

such times for God. Thus, Pike's argument would not work under a timeless viewpoint of the divine nature. Pike's argument would need to be revised to account for an atemporal understanding of the divine nature. In this case, an atemporal and omniscient God could know how he would choose to act logically prior to his choice. Logical priority is a non-temporal notion where things logically precede other things in order to provide a conceptual explanation of something. For example, my existence logically precedes my typing. I must exist logically prior to my typing in order to explain the action of my typing. As a result, God could know his own actions logically prior to willing those actions as a means of explaining why he acts the way he does. Since this reformulation appeals to logical priority instead of temporal priority, it removes the temporal notions in Pike's argument without losing the core notion that God's knowledge renders his choice and action unfree. If God's foreknowledge is logically prior to his action and explains his action, then God appears not to be free. Thus, the problem of foreknowledge and divine freedom remains for an atemporal God.

Zagzebski's Argument

Linda Zagzebski proposes another interesting version of the problem of foreknowledge and human freedom. Zagzebski claims that this version allows one to circumvent the issue of divine temporality. First, she assumes that one accepts the Principle of Accidental Necessity, where something that is either past or actual is now necessary. Second, one asserts the Principle of the Transfer of Necessity. This principle has two forms. Form (1) states:

(1) Necessarily p; necessarily (p implies q); therefore, necessarily q.

Form (2) states:

(2) Necessarily p; necessarily (p and q are equivalent); therefore, necessarily q.

If a necessary state of affairs either implies another state of affairs or is equivalent to another state of affairs, then necessity transfers from the former state of affairs to the latter. From these principles, one could argue that if God's knowledge of the future is accidentally necessary (is past or now actual), then no one does anything freely. Everyone would act of necessity. With S representing an action and t representing a time, the argument is as follows:

1. Necessarily, If God believes at t_1 that I will do S at t_3, then I do S at t_3.
2. It is accidentally necessary at t_2 that God believes at t_1 that I will do S at t_3. (necessity of the past or actuality)
3. If 1 and 2, then it is accidentally necessary at t_2 that I do S at t_3. (Transfer of Necessity (1))
4. It is accidentally necessary at t_2 that I do S at t_3.
5. If it is accidentally necessary at t_2 that I do S at t_3, then I do not do S at t_3 freely.
6. I do not do S at t_3 freely.

If one uses the second form of the Transfer of Necessity Principle, the first premise would read: Necessarily, if God believes at t_1 that I will do S at t_3, then I do S at t_3.[9] In short, if God knows that an agent will do an action in the future, then that agent must do that action or God would be fallible. Since God's state of knowledge is actual, that state is accidentally necessary and what God believes is accidentally necessary. That accidental necessity transfers from God's state of knowledge to the agent's future action since God's knowledge implies the agent's future action. Thus, the agent's future action is accidentally necessary, and he cannot act otherwise. If the agent cannot act otherwise, then the agent cannot be free.

Zagzebski continues by clarifying the definition of accidental necessity in three ways. First, accidental necessity attaches to contingent objects and states of affairs that once were not actualized but are now actualized. This is not to say that these objects and states of affairs are metaphysically necessary in that they could not have failed to exist. They are necessary only in the sense that once they obtain, they cannot have failed to obtain. Thus, the necessity is accidental to the obtaining of the object. These objects and states of affairs did not need to be actualized but now are actualized. Subsequently, their actualization cannot be undone. Accidental necessity exhibits a distinction between an object or state of affairs being actual or non-actual. Second, accidental necessity is dependent on an asymmetrical view of time: that time has a one-way direction and each temporal point is different from the previous point. Third, accidental necessity applies to states of affairs, not propositions.[10] Zagzebski believes that the necessity of the past cannot be transferred to the future since the future is not actualized in the manner the past is; however, some sort of necessity must be transferred. She calls this accidental ne-

---

9 Linda Zagzebski, *The Dilemma of Freedom and Foreknowledge* (Oxford University Press, 1991), 7–8.
10 Ibid., 15–21, 24, 26–28.

cessity*: a kind of necessity that some state of affairs p has when p is strictly implied by some accidentally necessary state of affairs q.[11]

With this understanding, Zagzebski forms a new version of the problem of foreknowledge and human freedom that she calls the Accidental Necessity Version: the accidentally necessary fact of God's knowledge is inconsistent with the contingency of some action and an agents' being free to perform it. There is also its cousin the Causal Necessity Version: given possible worlds, there are causal laws that causally necessitate what God knows, thus removing causal contingency and subsequently freedom.[12] Suppose I will do S at t_3 and that God believes at t_1 that I will do S at t_3. It follows on the Accidental Necessity Version:

1. God's belief at t_1 that I will do S at t_3 is accidentally necessary at t_2.
2. If A is accidentally necessary at t and A strictly implies B, then B is accidentally necessary* at t.
3. God's belief at t_1 strictly implies my act at t_3.
4. So my act at t_3 is accidentally necessary* at t_2.
5. If my act at t_3 is accidentally necessary* at t_2, I cannot do otherwise than bring about that act at t_3.
6. If when I bring about an act I cannot do otherwise, I do not bring it about freely.
7. Therefore, I do not bring about my act at t_3 freely.

The second form of the Transfer of Necessity Principle can replace premises 2 and 3 by changing strict implication to strict equivalence.[13] As before, God's state of knowledge is necessary and that necessity transfers to my future action since God's state of belief implies my future action. As a result, my action is necessary, and I cannot do otherwise.

Unlike Zagzebski, Michael Tooley believes that pure accidental necessity can apply to future states. Tooley offers the following principle.

(*) It is accidentally necessary that p at time t iff p is not preventable at time t.

---

11 Ibid., 30.
12 Ibid., 31–32.
13 Ibid., 36–37.

Tooley claims that this principle allows accidental necessity to transfer from the past to the future via the Transfer of Necessity Principle (1).[14] However, what does "preventable" mean? Tooley states

> (C) It is accidentally necessary that p at time t iff no being, either actual or possible, acting at time t, could causally bring it about that p is false.

So Zagzebski's accidental necessity* concept appears to be unnecessary since pure accidental necessity will suffice for the success of the argument.[15]

How does accidental necessity affect freedom? Since God's state of knowledge requires the actuality of some particular action by an agent, then that action is accidentally necessary and cannot be changed. The action, therefore, is not free. These arguments can apply to God as well. God's state of knowledge about the future, though logically contingent, is now either temporally or timelessly actual; therefore, that state is accidentally necessary since it obtains. If God's state of knowledge strictly implies his knowledge of divine choices and actions temporally or logically prior to their actualization, then God's choices and actions are also accidentally necessary by transfer of necessity. God, therefore, is not free to choose and to act. He can act only as his accidentally necessary state of knowledge directs him to act. Since God's state of knowledge regarding his future actions is actual, those actions are accidentally necessary. Any implications of that divine state are also necessary by transfer of necessity whether those implications exist in time or not. God's particular choices and actions do not seem to be preventable given his accidentally necessary divine state of knowledge.

Examining Divine Freedom

As the preceding arguments show, God does not seem to be a free being given his knowledge of the future. If God's omniscient nature requires knowledge of the future, then God seems to know his own choices and actions temporally or logically prior to performing them. God then would be a determined being, and he does not seem to be free. Such arguments concerning the issue of divine freedom and foreknowledge are not necessarily new. Richard LaCroix makes a similar claim. LaCroix argues for the following principles:

---

14 Michael Tooley, "Freedom and Foreknowledge," *FP* 17 (2000): 218–219.
15 Ibid., 220–221.

(P1) For any act that God performs, there is no time prior to that act at which God does not know that he will perform that act.

(P2) If God knows at t_1 that he will do (will not do) a at t_3, then at t_1 or t_2 it is not possible for God to refrain from doing (to do) a at t_3.[16]

LaCroix claims that divine foreknowledge of the future implies (P1) and that the falsity of (P1) is contrary to foreknowledge. God would perform an act that he did not know about at some prior time to the act. If (P2) is false, then LaCroix argues that God can know at t_1 that he will do a at t_3 and that he can refrain from doing a at t_3. However, God should know at t_1 that he will refrain at t_3 rather than that he will act. As a result, God knows at t_1 that he both will and will not do a at t_3. This conclusion is contradictory since both cannot be known at the same time; therefore, God must know and do a at t_3. LaCroix claims that both of his principles are required of foreknowledge. LaCroix also argues from these claims that God cannot decide-choose-purpose to perform the acts that he does perform. LaCroix argues that decisions are typically in time and involve deliberation to reach a conclusion. Decisions involve future actions about which one is uncertain what to do, and they involve genuine alternatives to act or to refrain. God cannot make any decisions based upon the above principles because he knows what he will do before he decides what he shall do. Thus, God cannot deliberate, he cannot be uncertain about the future, and he does not have any genuine alternatives. All of these things are consistent with the claims of foreknowledge. God, therefore, cannot decide to refrain or refrain at all. He has no freedom.[17]

Philip Quinn, however, points out problems with LaCroix's arguments. LaCroix claims that if God knows at t_1 that he will do a at t_3, then it is not possible at t_2 for God to refrain from doing a at t_3. Quinn notes that if this claim is contradictory and false, then both the antecedent and the consequent of LaCroix's claim will be true: that is God knows at t_1 that he will do a at t_3, and it is possible at t_2 for God to refrain from doing a at t_3. These counter claims, however, only generate the claim that it is possible that God does a at t_3 and that it is possible that God does not do a at t_3. Neither of these are contradictory nor are they a necessary falsehood; therefore, it seems possible that God can either do or not do a at t_3.[18] Quinn states that in order for LaCroix's argument to work, LaCroix needs to claim that it is necessary that God will do a

---

16 Richard LaCroix, "Omniprescience and Divine Determinism," *RS* 12 (1976): 369–370.
17 Ibid., 370–374.
18 Philip Quinn, "Divine Foreknowledge and Divine Freedom," *IJPR* 9 (1978): 223–225.

at t_3 in order to show that it is impossible that God will refrain from doing a at t_3. Thus, Quinn believes a theist may maintain that God foreknows what he will do while maintaining that God could refrain, though to be sure God will not refrain.[19]

Quinn also asserts that it is also possible that there is a first moment of time when God made all of his decisions. If this were so, there would never have been a previous time in which God did not know what he would do at a later time. As a result, there may not be a time prior to t_2 in which an agent does not know what he is going to do at t_3. Quinn argues that one would have to assume infinite time for LaCroix's argument to work, but even then, one can only assert that God could have intended at every time prior to t_2 to do a at t_3. In fact, Quinn argues that God can know at t_1 that he will decide at t_2 to do a at t_3. One can then infer that God has not decided at t_1 to do a at t_3, and he knows at t_1 that he will do a at t_3. Quinn sees nothing that is illogical about this latter conclusion but admits it seems odd.[20]

Quinn goes on to argue that God may not decide at any particular time but may eternally intend at all times. Although God's mind would always be made up and fixed, this does not demonstrate that it is necessary that God have the intentions and foreknowledge that he possesses. God's intentions and foreknowledge could have been different, so God could have refrained. In fact, God could so intend and then not do what he intends if one rejects the notions of perfect goodness and infallibility. No law of logic or nature constrains God so that God's intention and action could not be different. LaCroix's argument does not show that God cannot act in this way.[21] Unfortunately, Quinn provides no explanation for how God's eternal intentions could be different than they are. Without such an explanation, it is not clear that they could be different. Further, his assertion that one could reject perfect goodness and divine infallibility to maintain divine freedom is rather extreme not to mention contradictory to the definition of omniscience provided in the second chapter as well as orthodox theology.

Tomis Kapitan assesses the claims that LaCroix and Quinn make. Kapitan notes that what LaCroix's argument entails is that there is a time t_1 prior to t_3 at which God does know and does not know at t_1 that he will decide to do a at t_2. Thus, God cannot choose or decide to do any action. Kapitan further notes that Quinn's argument that one can know at t_1 what he will decide at t_2 is ambiguous. Basically, one can know beforehand what he will decide or

---

19 Ibid., 228.
20 Ibid., 230–234.
21 Ibid., 236–238.

intend at a later time only because he has already decided or intended. One is merely rehearsing his previous decision or intention.[22] Kapitan goes on to argue that a deliberator who is trying to make decisions only does so if he believes that he has open alternatives; however, one can know what he will decide without knowing that an alternative action is open. The alternative may be a possible action, but it is not open to the agent. Kapitan claims that an event or proposition is open and contingent so long as it or its negation is not the consequence of a certain state of affairs. The state of affairs must not be sufficient for the obtaining of the event or proposition, and this sufficiency may also be causal in nature.[23]

According to Kapitan, a deliberator does not yet know what he will decide because of this open alternative. He has a sense of uncertainty in choosing from a plurality of options. Because of this uncertainty, no agent could know what he will decide at any time prior to the decision. Even if God made his decisions at the first moment of time, this situation would indicate that at the time God both did and did not know what he had decided if he considers his choice open. If God decides all his actions from the first moment of time, then he does not consider them open, and he never decided them. If all possible actions are open from the first moment of time, then Quinn's argument fails.[24] If God does know what he will decide at any time prior to the decision, then he does not consider that decision contingent and open. It is closed. Thus, God would not have free choice, but this closure does not imply that God is logically determined since he could have known or intended otherwise.[25]

Richard Taylor also agrees with Kapitan. Taylor argues that a person can only deliberate about his own possible actions. He cannot deliberate about the possible actions of others. He can only deliberate about his own future actions since past and present ones already exist and can no longer be deliberated over. Deliberation is not like speculation. One cannot deliberate about a future action that one already believes to be inevitable because the agent no longer believes the action is within his power to perform or forego. One cannot deliberate about what he will do while at the same time knowing what he is going to do. One can know what one will do only by inference or by decision. If an agent's will is caused by antecedent conditions, then he could infer what he will do by knowing those causes. Deliberation, therefore, rests on not knowing the outcome beforehand. If one deliberates about an action

---

22 Tomis Kapitan, "Can God Make Up His Mind?" *IJPR* 15 (1984): 37–39.
23 Ibid., 40–41.
24 Ibid., 42–44.
25 Ibid., 44–45.

that is caused but is ignorant of that causation, then his deliberation is pointless. If a person does not know what he is going to do but knows that certain conditions are already in place sufficient to cause whatever it is he is going to do, then that person cannot deliberate. He can only guess or speculate.[26] Taylor concludes that no one, not even God, can know the forthcomings of deliberations. If God does foreknow deliberations, then he has inferred it from causal conditions or the decision has been declared, both of which signal an absence of deliberation.[27]

The theory of divine ideas, however, does not appear to indicate that God's choices and actions are open, contingent, and able to be otherwise. As a result, God could not be a deliberator. These choices and actions are components of the divine ideas, which are part of the divine nature. The ideas have always been fixed in their content, and their content cannot be different. If the divine ideas are fixed and dictate what God will decide concerning either creation or his actions within creation, then God knows the outcome of those choices temporally or logically prior to making them. Thus, God cannot consider the alternatives to those choices open to him. God would be determined by his nature; therefore, God could not be a deliberator. God's perfect goodness could also necessitate that God act in a certain manner in a certain situation. Thus, God cannot deliberate over those choices, and they would not be open for God. The theory of divine ideas, therefore, presents a problem concerning the extent of the divine freedom. If God's choices are fixed and closed by the divine ideas, then God appears to be neither a deliberator nor a free being. Thus, the problem of divine freedom remains.

Are Kapitan and Taylor's claims correct? Bruce Reichenbach believes they are partially incorrect. Reichenbach agrees that one cannot deliberate about the past. One only deliberates about what he may do. An agent weighs options and deliberates about what he perceives to be in his power to perform. As a result, he also believes in some indeterminacy. Agents deliberate about how to act, and the agent deliberates to make up his mind to do that which is best in accord with his beliefs, desires, and intentions.[28] Reichenbach argues that Taylor's argument commits a fallacy by saying that the possibility of knowing one's deliberations removes one's ability to deliberate. Reichenbach argues that just because one *could* know the outcome of his deliberation does not mean that he can no longer deliberate. The agent, however, must actually know the outcome of his deliberation, and then he cannot deliberate. Also,

---

26 Richard Taylor, "Deliberation and Foreknowledge," *APQ* 1 (1964): 73–76.
27 Ibid., 78–79.
28 Bruce Reichenbach, "Omniscience and Deliberation," *IJPR* 16 (1984): 225–227.

such knowledge cannot be communicated to the agent and that agent still deliberate. Reichenbach concedes that if God foreknows his choices, then he certainly cannot deliberate.[29] Since God seems to know how he will choose in some if not all circumstances according to the theory of divine ideas, then it follows that God cannot deliberate in those circumstances and cannot be free.

On the other hand, Reichenbach believes that God can still act intentionally because intention does not necessitate deliberation. Intentions can be either spontaneous or routine. Reichenbach thinks that such intentional and purposive actions that do not involve deliberation exist, such as driving the fastest way to work or providing a thirsty child with water. There are also two senses of the word "decision." The first is when one initiates an action in correspondence with desires and goals. The second is when one deliberates out of uncertainty. As a result, Reichenbach rejects the argument that all decision-making involves uncertain deliberation. First, Reichenbach rejects the sense of "decision" used by the argument. Second, the argument only accounts for intentions derived from decision-making, but some intentional actions are not derived in this manner. God cannot deliberate, but that does not mean that he does not act intentionally.[30] God's choices and actions may be determined but can still be intentional and free.

David Basinger contends that Reichenbach's argument assumes that all intentional action is non-deliberative from a divine standpoint; however, Reichenbach has shown that only some divine intentional actions are non-deliberative. Basinger argues that most theists would not accept Reichenbach's view. Instead, they would hold that God does deliberate in examples such as

---

29 Ibid., 229.

30 Ibid., 230–233. The argument that all decision making involves not knowing what will occur is made by Carl Ginet. Ginet argues that it is conceptually impossible to know one's decision before one makes it. A person can know his decision beforehand only by knowing causal relations related to that decision. It is simply logically inconsistent, however, to state that one knows what he will later decide to do. Such claims imply that a decision has already been made, which is illogical. Decision thus implies ignorance. On the other hand, J. W. Roxbee Cox claims that Ginet is wrong. One does learn something, namely that one has decided and that one's prior claim to foreknowledge was borne out. It is not necessary, however, to learn anything new about what one is going to do or will decide to do, though this is normally what happens. Cox believes that claiming that deciding is a way of gaining knowledge is misleading, since it would imply that discovering a certain decision will be made and actually making that decision are competing methods of gaining the same knowledge. Thus, it is misleading to state that the aim of making up one's mind leads to a kind of certainty. Making up one's mind is knowledge of what to do, which is not the same as knowledge of what we will do. See Carl Ginet, "Can the Will be Caused?" *PR* 71 (1962): 50–52; Stuart Hampshire and H. L. A. Hart, "Decision, Intention, and Certainty," *Mind* 67 (1958): 1–12; J. W. Roxbee Cox, "Can I Know Beforehand What I Am Going to Decide?" *PR* 72 (1963): 88.

whether to create or answer prayers. Basinger notes that Reichenbach's position denies indeterminate and free action of God. If God never deliberates but acts only according to intentions and goals he already has in mind, then there is no moment chronologically or logically in which God has decided what should occur. Two creative options were never both equally open. God has simply initiated what he already knew he wanted to be actual.[31] Basinger has a point. All of God's choices could be closed and non-deliberative. If God cannot deliberate between alternatives, then he seems to have merely initiated what he was predisposed to desire rather than having decided what he wanted. Thus, God does not appear to be free.

Except for Reichenbach, most of these philosophers assume divine freedom in the libertarian sense; thus, their arguments only work if this position is correct. What if libertarian freedom is not real? What if God possesses compatibilist freedom instead of libertarian freedom? God not knowing the outcome of his choices until he decides would not be an issue. God knowing the outcome of his choices prior to making them or by being unable to deliberate would not mean a loss of freedom since compatibilist free will is compatible with such non-deliberative determinism. This conception of God's freedom is possible.

The concept in mind here is similar to that of the Best Possible World Theory as developed by G. W. Leibniz. While contending with the question as to why evil exists in the world, Leibniz argued that God, being perfectly good, must create that world which is the best. He cannot create any other world that is less than the best possible. Should God create such a world less than the best possible, then he would not be perfect because he would have done something inferior. Leibniz concludes then that the actual world must be the best possible world even though it contains evil; therefore, God cannot be held responsible for the evil within the world that he created.[32]

Appealing to Leibniz' argument, all of God's choices of what world to create to what actions to perform within that world could be determined by the divine nature and its causal implications. Since this conception would be incompatible with libertarian freedom, compatibilist freedom could be substituted in order to avoid the problem of foreknowledge and divine freedom. God's nature would determine God's choices and actions. Subsequently, God would intend to follow that determination so that all his choices and actions

---

31 David Basinger, "Omniscience and Deliberation: A Reply to Reichenbach," *IJPR* 20 (1986): 170–171.

32 G. W. Leibniz, *Theodicy*, ed. Austin Farrer, trans. E. M. Huggard (Open Court, 1990). For a shorter version of this argument, see G. W. Leibniz, *Discourse on Metaphysics*, trans. George Montgomery (Dover Publication Company, 2005), I–VI.

correspond with his nature as Reichenbach argues. Edward Wierenga has even argued something similar to these claims.[33]

Although Wes Morriston takes issue with this line of argumentation, he claims that there is some initial plausibility to this view. All causal factors for determined choices are internal to God rather than being external to him as traditional compatibilist freedom contends. Thus, all of God's choices are determined by factors internal to him rather than being determined by factors external to him. Despite this claim, Morriston believes this claim to be insufficient to guarantee freedom. God is stuck by his nature and cannot choose contrary to it. Thus, God's nature is the ultimate determiner of divine choice rather than God's will.[34] Still, this conclusion might not be troubling if compatibilist free will is real and one is willing to accept it. It would not matter that God's nature determines his choice. God could still have freedom but only in the compatibilist sense.

A troubling consequence of this view is that it implies that some form of fatalism is true. Since God would be determined by his nature to create one and only one specific world, then that world is the only world that God can logically create. All other worlds would be logically impossible for him to create. Thus, God is logically fated to create that world (the actual world) which is determined by his nature. This fatalism would trickle down to all other aspects of reality as well. Not only would God's actions be fated but also the actions of all other created agents would be fated as well. In order to avoid making God a fated being, at least one of God's choices, the choice of whether and what to create, would need to be undetermined. As a result, God must have libertarian freedom in at least this one choice to escape fatalism. God could still be considered free even if all of the other divine choices remained determined if one is willing to accept compatibilist freedom as a viable notion.

If divine libertarian freedom must be correct to avoid fatalism, then compatibilist freedom does not appear to be the best understanding of divine freedom. If determined divine desires that lead to determined divine choices are not sufficient to guarantee divine freedom rather than fatalism, then the notion of divine compatibilist freedom in all choices collapses. In order to be free and not fated, God needs the ability to do otherwise. Compatibilist freedom, therefore, cannot be sufficient for divine freedom. Because libertarian freedom provides the ability to do otherwise, it appears to be the best notion of freedom that is applicable to God. If this is the case, the question of the compatibility between foreknowledge and divine libertarian freedom fol-

---

33 Edward Wierenga, "The Freedom of God," *FP* 19, no. 4 (2002): 425–436.
34 Wes Morriston, "Is God Free: Reply to Wierenga," *FP* 23 (2006): 95–97.

lows. How can God have the ability to do otherwise if he foreknows his own future actions and must perform them? Perhaps foreknowledge is inimical to divine freedom, and the idea should be abandoned bringing a change to the definition of omniscience. If not, how can God know the future if he could always do otherwise? If God is not constrained in his ability to choose and act, then he could do anything he wishes at any moment within the actual world. If so, then how can God know with certainty what will transpire in the future? He may know what could happen based upon his choice, but he cannot know what will happen since he has not yet chosen. The future is in limbo until God actually chooses. If God knows the future temporally or logically prior to any of his choices, then it seems that his choices must be determined so that he can know the future with certainty prior to making his choices. As a result, it seems that God's foreknowledge require that he not have libertarian freedom. The question then is how God can have both the libertarian freedom and the determined foreknowledge temporally or logically prior to his own choices.

Assessment

The problem of foreknowledge and divine freedom is fraught with the same difficulties as the problem of foreknowledge and human freedom. On one hand, there is the desire to give God power over all of his alternatives so that he may enact any one of them and be a real deliberator of open options rather than a fated being. On the other hand, there is the desire to uphold God's perfection as well as God's omniscience. Since the conception of omniscience outlined in the first chapter implies that God is able to know the future and it is clear that God must possess libertarian freedom to avoid fatalism, then the problem of foreknowledge and divine freedom needs to be resolved to understand the nature of the divine freedom and its relationship with divine omniscience.

As a means to solve this difficulty, I will look for a solution among the different theories that have been applied to the human side of the foreknowledge and freedom problem. In the following chapters, I explore different ways of resolving the problem of foreknowledge and human freedom and apply these positions to the divine situation. Each position will be criticized and rejected if it is found wanting. At the end of this study, I will arrive at what I consider to be the solution to the problem of foreknowledge and divine freedom. As a consequence of accepting libertarian freedom and the ability of God to do otherwise, I will not consider any position on the problem of foreknowledge and human freedom that rejects this definition of freedom.

I propose to examine each theory according to the following criteria. First, a successful solution will avoid logical fatalism and allow for some level of ultimate contingency. Logical fatalism is the position that there is only one logically possible outcome to reality. As a result, all things in existence are logically necessary, and there is no contingency. Logical fatalism is not only at odds with the common-sense notion of logical possibility but it also completely obliterates free agency of any kind. In order to preserve the realities of possibility, contingency, and free agency, not all truths can be necessary truths. I assume here that God is a logically necessary being rather than a contingent being since nothing is above or beyond God that can determine that he exist or not exist. As a result, God must be free in order to avoid logical fatalism. Any solution to the problem of foreknowledge and divine freedom must avoid logical fatalism.

Second, a successful solution will conclude that God is not constrained by natural necessity. God is traditionally defined as a perfectly good being who may only do what is morally good. As a perfectly good being, God's actions could be completely determined by this aspect of his nature as Leibniz contends; however, such a conclusion implies that all of God's actions are naturally necessary rather than some being contingent. Thus, God is unable to act in any manner different from what his perfectly good nature dictates in a given situation. As a result, it is logically impossible for God to do other than what his nature implies. This position, along with the position that God is a logically necessary being, implies logical fatalism. If God is a logically necessary being and is naturally necessitated to create a specific world and to perform specific actions in that world, then such a position implies logical fatalism. God's logically necessary existence implies his naturally necessary action with its naturally necessary effect. If God is a contingent being, however, then it would be logically possible for God and his nature not to exist along with the naturally necessary divine action and its effects. God, however, cannot be a contingent being since there is nothing that can determine whether or not God exists. However one puts it, if God is logically unable to do other than what his nature implies in any given situation, then God is not free in that situation. These implications are inimical to free agency. It could be said, however, that while God is not naturally necessitated to create a specific world, he could be so necessitated in other situations due to his perfect goodness, making him unfree only in those situations. A successful solution to the problem of foreknowledge and divine freedom, therefore, will avoid natural necessity in some crucial cases of divine action.

Third, a successful solution must be consistent with the theory of omniscient foreknowledge based on the theory of divine ideas as established in chapter one. The theory of divine ideas implies that certain divine actions are part of the history of certain possible worlds. Those actions are necessary in order for a specific possible world to obtain. If God wills to actualize a world strongly, then he must also actualize a certain history, which includes divine actions, to ensure that this world obtains. If he fails to obtain that history and perform those actions, then the possible world, along with the divine will, fail to obtain. Since the divine will cannot fail to obtain, these divine actions must be actualized by God. The theory of divine ideas could imply a type of necessity of the divine action; however, this implication depends on how each individual theory deals with the divine ideas. Since this study assumes the theory of divine ideas is the correct position regarding the nature of divine omniscience, a successful solution to the problem of foreknowledge and divine freedom will be able to incorporate successfully this theory without depriving God of freedom. I shall judge the merit of any potential solution to the problem of foreknowledge and divine freedom based on these criteria. With this set of criteria in place, the search for a solution begins.

Chapter 3

The Open Solution

Having established the problem of foreknowledge and divine freedom in the second chapter, this study now turns to exploring potential ways to overcome this problem. In chapters one and two, I argued that God is omniscient, and he is able to know the future. If God knows the future, then he should know his own future choices and actions. If foreknowledge is incompatible with freedom, then God's freedom is called into question. Since the problem of foreknowledge and human freedom follows this same scheme, this study seeks to solve the problem of foreknowledge and divine freedom by focusing on those positions that have been proposed to resolve the human side of the problem.

This chapter deals with the Open Solution. The Open Solution embraces the claim that foreknowledge and freedom are incompatible. As a result, it rejects the claim that God possesses knowledge of the future. Though there are some aspects of the future that can be known (such as things that are either logically or naturally necessary) God does not know future contingents. God, therefore, does not know the free actions of either human beings or himself. In this chapter, I explicate the Open position and its four variations: Voluntary Nescience, Involuntary Nescience, Non-Bivalent Omniscience, and Bivalent Omniscience. I argue that Bivalent Omniscience is the best version and apply its claims to the divine situation. Lastly, I argue that this version of the Open Solution fails to dismiss the problem of foreknowledge and divine freedom.

The Open View of the Future

The Open Solution, also known as Open Theism, argues that loving relationship is God's primary quality. For Open Theism, love is defined as care, commitment, sensitivity, and response to others. This propensity to love implies that God's relationship with his created creatures follows this scheme. Open Theism also asserts that God must have a real relationship with his creation, which cannot be accomplished if human beings are not free beings. As a result, Open Theists accept Pike's argument and claim that foreknowledge is not compatible with freedom. If God knows the future, then human beings would not be free and all relationships would be illusory. Open Theists also claim that moral responsibility would be an illusion because God would be the source of all evil. Thus, God's knowledge and actions must be conditioned by creation, particularly by free creatures, in order for there to be a real relationship.

To support this view, Open Theists point to specific biblical passages where God expresses surprise or regret over certain actions he has taken. In Gen 6:6–7, God is said to be grieved that he created man. This passage suggests that God hoped things would have been different from the way they occurred. This claim is also asserted of 1 Sam 15:11, 35, where God is grieved that he made Saul king of Israel. Other passages seem to suggest that God is able to change his mind. In Gen 18:20–33, Abraham negotiates with God over saving Sodom and Gomorrah from destruction, and in 2 Kgs 20:1–20, God relents and does not let Hezekiah die as God previously stated would happen. It is argued that these passages should be interpreted literally rather than anthropomorphically.[1] If God is surprised by what transpires or can change his mind, then God cannot possess exhaustive knowledge of the future.

Open Theists, such as Clark Pinnock, argue that it is false to claim that an omnipotent God must have complete control over any world he creates. He argues that sovereignty only indicates that God has the ability to create any world he wishes. God could create a world that he controls in meticulous fashion, but he is not compelled to do so. He could create a world that owes its existence to him but does not conform to his intentions and values. Existence is a gift from God, and God only has those limits that he places on himself. Since God can create a world with some degree of self-regulation, he does not need a monopoly on power. As a result, God voluntarily limits his

---

1 Millard Erickson, *What Does God Know and When Does He Know It?* (Zondervan, 2003), 17–38; Gregory Boyd, *God of the Possible* (Baker Books, 2000), 54–85; idem, "The Open Theism View," in *Divine Foreknowledge: Four Views,* ed. James Beilby and Paul Eddy (InterVarsity Press, 2001), 23–24; Clark Pinnock, *Most Moved Mover* (Baker Academic, 2001), 47–53. Pinnock goes so far as to suggest that the claim of foreknowledge is the result of pagan influences on the Church (*Most Moved Mover*, 65–79).

control. Instead, God can anticipate what will happen and plan accordingly so that his purposes, in general, will be accomplished.[2]

This appeal to sovereignty is juxtaposed with the claim that there must be human freedom. The Bible asserts that human agents are sinners who can freely respond to God in love or who can deliberately reject God's plan for them; therefore, human freedom must exist. Open Theists claim that freedom is restricted by certain variables, such as with whom one interacts, with what one interacts, the past, and oneself. However, agents are not wholly shaped by external factors. God wants a world where creatures may express real love and participate in real relationships. Such qualities can only exist if creatures are free to perform them, Open Theists claim. No agent could express these qualities if he is fixed to act in a certain way; therefore, freedom requires that agents be able to do otherwise, not to be controlled either externally or internally.[3] If human beings have such libertarian freedom, God would take this freedom into account in his rule of the world. God would not cling to his right to dominate but would allow his creatures room to act. Thus, God refrains from expressing some of his power in order to have a real, loving relationship with human beings. God does not use a blueprint that fixes everything into place. Instead, God's plan of relationship is flexible and responsive to what happens.[4]

As a result, Open Theists believe that God takes risks. He makes plans and decisions whose outcomes depend on the response of libertarianly free beings. These responses are not known since such knowledge is not available to God. Such responses may be contrary to God's wishes and intentions causing God's work to be hindered. Since God has endowed human beings with libertarian freedom, free will responses by his creatures are not causally determined and are inherently indeterministic. This freedom guarantees the ability to decide between genuine alternatives; otherwise, freedom and true agency would be an illusion, and human personhood would be undermined. As a result, God can only have probable knowledge of future contingent ac-

---

[2] Clark Pinnock, "God Limits His Knowledge," in *Predestination and Free Will: Four Views on Divine Sovereignty and Human Freedom*, ed. David and Randall Basinger (InterVarsity Press, 1986), 145–147.

[3] Ibid., 147–149; Gregory Boyd, "God Limits His Control," in *Four Views on Divine Providence*, ed. Stanley Gundry (Zondervan, 2011), 188–190.

[4] Pinnock, "God Limits His Knowledge," 151–152; Boyd, "God Limits His Control," 190–192. Boyd describes this free interaction between God and his creation in terms of a war against the forces of evil. See Boyd's *God at War* (InterVarsity Press, 1997) and *Satan and the Problem of Evil* (InterVarsity Press, 2001).

tions and events. Since God does not know future contingent actions and events with certainty, God puts himself at risk of failure.[5]

Open Theists argue that foreknowledge and exhaustive sovereignty undermine God's glory. If God must completely control things, then God cannot create a world where he does not control all things, which appears detrimental to his power and glory. Thus, God's omnipotence is limited because his choices are limited. The necessity of foreknowledge suggests the need for complete control and therefore a limited God. Further, even if God should choose to completely control all things, this choice cannot be praiseworthy. Praiseworthiness comes from character and good moral action. A God who chooses not to exercise all the power he could and who lovingly responds to his creation as it changes is praiseworthy. A God who chooses to express all the power that he could and fixes everything a certain way is not praiseworthy. It seems that he is manipulative and tyrannical. Open Theists contend that both power and morality are grounded in choice, not control.[6] As a result, agents must have the ability to act freely once given the gift of freedom, and God must endure the misuses of that freedom so that it may be a genuine gift.[7] Instead, Open Theists claim that God is like a wise chess master. The chess master does not possess a blueprint of his opponent's moves to ensure a win. Instead, he knows all of the possible moves of his opponent and is wise and confident enough to anticipate his opponent's moves. He may even have to risk certain pieces in order to win, but it is his superior wisdom that is praiseworthy rather than an ability to control his opponent. God, therefore, is like the wise chess master because of his perfect knowledge of all possibilities.[8] He can win no matter what free creatures do.

Alan Rhoda defines Open Theism's philosophical premises as these: (1) the future is causally open such that it is possible that x obtains or that x does not obtain at some future time, and (2) the future is epistemically open such

---

[5] William Hasker, "God Takes Risks," in *Contemporary Debates in Philosophy of Religion*, ed. Michael Peterson and Raymond VanArragon (Blackwell Publishing, 2004), 219; Boyd, *Satan and the Problem of Evil*, 88–92; Pinnock, *The Most Moved Mover*, 100–102.

[6] Boyd, *Satan and the Problem of Evil*, 148–151; Richard Rice, *God's Foreknowledge and Man's Free Will* (Bethany House Publishers, 1985), 25–31, 42, 53–58, 63–65; John Sanders, "God as Personal," in *The Grace of God, the Will of Man*, ed. Clark Pinnock (Zondervan, 1989), 165–180; John Sanders, *The God Who Risks* (InterVarsity, 1998), 169–172; David Basinger, *The Case For Freewill Theism* (InterVarsity, 1996), 33–36; Pinnock, *Most Moved Mover*, 47–53.

[7] Ibid., 181–182, 183n6, 191, 420. Boyd calls this a covenant of non-coercion. God will not micromanage human choices because of the freedom given to human beings. However, God can intervene once one has surpassed certain limits because God is not obliged to let agents always do as they choose.

[8] Boyd, *Satan and the Problem of Evil*, 113–114; Rice, *God's Foreknowledge and Man's Free Will*, 66–67.

The Open Solution 59

that a person *S* at any time *t* with respect to some state of affairs *x* does not know either that *x* will obtain at some future time or that *x* will not obtain at some future time. The future is not causally fixed, and no one can know what will occur in the future. The first premise is logically prior to the second. It must be impossible to know the future to the extent that it is causally open; therefore, the future cannot be epistemically settled for God in any respect in which it is causally open. The content of God's knowledge changes over time as things are no longer future and are no longer causally open. God's nature does not change, but his beliefs, will, and emotions are subject to change.[9] Rhoda further claims that Open Theists, while staunch regarding epistemic openness of the future, differ regarding the alethic openness of the future. Alethic openness is the view that not every proposition about future events has a truth value. As a result, Rhoda claims that there are several different versions of Open Theism. Limited Foreknowledge (what I term Voluntary and Involuntary Nescience) argues that future contingents are alethically settled but epistemically unknowable for certain reasons. Those who emphasize a particular understanding of the principle of bivalence (or Bivalent Omniscience) argue that future contingents are alethically open because statements about future contingents are false. Those who reject bivalence (or Non-Bivalent Omniscience) argue that future contingents are alethically open because statements about the future have no truth value.[10]

Versions of the Open View

This chapter now turns to examining these different positions in light of the problem with foreknowledge and divine freedom. Since the Open View at its core argues that foreknowledge must be denied in order for real freedom to exist, then God's freedom seems to require that he not foreknow his future. If God does not know what he will choose until he has chosen, then his future is to some extent open and not causally determined. God has the libertarian freedom to choose or refrain from choosing any particular option. Can any of these various theories dismiss the problem of foreknowledge and divine freedom? To answer this question, the best version of the Open View must be determined. In the following section, I explain each of the various Open Theist positions. After examining each Open Theist position, I assess criticisms against each position and conclude that the best position is Bivalent

---

9   Alan Rhoda, "Generic Open Theism and Some Varieties Thereof," *RS* 44 (2008): 226–228.
10 Ibid., 229.

Omniscience. I then apply the claims of this position to the divine situation in order to dismiss the problem of foreknowledge and divine freedom.

Voluntary Nescience

Voluntary Nescience was first introduced on the contemporary philosophical and theological scene by Richard Swinburne.[11] Swinburne begins his argument by explaining free choice. A free action has no full explanation of any kind. If an action happened because of a person's brain state, his genetics, or his upbringing, then that person would not be responsible for his action because he could not have done otherwise. Such physical states would constitute a necessity of some sort that disavows praise or blame since the agent could not do otherwise. The agent is not the ultimate source of responsibility and therefore not free. Swinburne argues that the same can be said of God's freedom. God's actions result from his intentional choices, and they have no full explanation. Thus, any person not influenced in his choices by causal factors is a free person.[12] Swinburne also notes that all actions are done for a reason, and all reasons are based on the judgment that something is good and worth doing. God certainly must act according to reasons and purposes. A perfectly free agent, like God, will never act irrationally. Further, such an agent will never perform an action for which he has an overriding reason to refrain or which he agrees would be worse to do than to refrain. Only rational factors can influence him.[13]

Swinburne believes that the traditional principle of omniscience with its knowledge of the future is possible; however, it cannot be true because it denies perfect freedom. Swinburne claims that a perfectly free agent can make a person's beliefs about a future state false, so the future cannot be known. Also, an omniscient being must know that a person A is free. Since A's actions are not caused by anything in the past, then an omniscient being's beliefs about A's actions must have a correlation with those actions. This conclusion suggests that A's actions caused these foreknown beliefs. Swinburne be-

---

11 Swinburne no longer advocates the Voluntary Nescience position as it has been edited from the revised edition of his work. His revised position is that God could know the future but has voluntarily limited himself in knowing the future by choosing to create free creatures. Since these free creatures' choices logically cannot be foreknown, then God logically cannot know the future. Thus, God's lack of knowledge concerning the future is a result of his own choosing of what type of creatures to create.

12 Richard Swinburne, *The Coherence of Theism* (Clarendon Press, 1977), 142–145; idem, *The Coherence of Theism*, rev. ed. (Clarendon Press, 1993), 146–149. Swinburne here defends the libertarian view of free will.

13 Ibid., 145–148; rev. ed., 149–152.

lieves this conclusion implies backwards causation, which is incoherent. An omniscient being, therefore, cannot be justified in holding beliefs about the future actions of a perfectly free agent. Consequently, an omniscient being cannot himself be perfectly free given this conception of omniscience. An omniscient being who knows everything that he will do prior to acting is possible, but that being could not be perfectly free. In order to allow for freedom, Swinburne argues that God must choose to limit his knowledge of what free creatures will choose to do. Further, God can free himself of this limitation at any moment by withdrawing free will.[14]

Swinburne accepts that all propositions, including those about the future, must have a truth value. On the other hand, God can be omniscient and can know all that is logically possible to know. Swinburne defines omniscience as knowing everything except for those future states that are not necessitated by current or past causal factors. Further, omniscience includes knowing that one is ignorant of those future states. A being can be perfectly free only by not knowing his future actions and their results. How does God possess this omniscience and freedom if it is possible for him to know the future? Swinburne argues that this omniscience and freedom result from God's own choice to preserve his freedom. God deliberately limits his own knowledge of the future to preserve his freedom and the freedom of others via a voluntary act of power.[15] In other words, God chooses to not know or to forget certain things about the future.

This position has also been attributed to Dallas Willard. John Sanders claims that Willard espouses dispositional omniscience which is similar to dispositional omnipotence. Just as God can do all things but chooses not to, God can know all things but chooses not to. God voluntarily limits his omniscience.[16] Gilbert Bilezikian also argues that if God is omniscient and knows all points of time, then he cannot be unaware of the future for he has total mastery and perspective of time. To respect creaturely freedom and not interfere with it, God can voluntary limit his awareness of creatures' actions. God can shelter this knowledge from the fullness of his omniscience; therefore, God can selectively limit his knowledge.[17] John Tal Murphree suggests that

---

14 Ibid., 166, 170–172; rev. ed., 174–177, 181–183.

15 Ibid., 175–178.

16 John Sanders, "On Heffalumps and Heresies: Responses to Accusations against Open Theism," *JBS* 2 (2002): 6–7; idem, "Be Wary of Ware: A Reply to Bruce Ware," *JETS* 45 (2002): 223. Sanders appeals to a personal letter from Dallas Willard in the footnotes. He also appeals to Willard's *The Divine Conspiracy* (Harper Collins, 1998), 244–246. This work, however, does not specifically argue for this position. Willard does deny that God has a cosmic stare where he must know all things whether he wants to or not.

17 Gilbert Bilezikian, *Christianity 101* (Zondervan, 1993), 29.

this voluntary action can be understood in the distinction between knowledge and consciousness. This position is like that of occurrent versus dispositional knowledge. A person can possess knowledge but not currently be conscious of that knowledge. Murphree argues that knowledge of something does not entail consciousness of that thing. Whether God is always conscious of everything that he knows is a different question from whether he always knows something. God could possess all knowledge, even of future contingencies, but choose not to be conscious of those facts. God does not lack knowledge. He is only currently unaware of some of the facts that he knows. God has perfect mental control such that he can block out things that he does not wish his mind to rest upon. This control is part of his omnipotent power.[18]

In the end, Voluntary Nescience includes the claim that God as an omniscient being does know the future. His knowledge of the future is both alethically settled and epistemically available. To preserve his own freedom as well as human freedom, God makes the decision and exercises the power to limit, block, or forget those truths within his epistemic power. Perhaps God simply refuses to consciously dwell on or remember those truths. Perhaps he completely deletes such knowledge from his mind. Whichever procedure he follows, those truths are no longer considered part of the epistemic range of the divine mind. Both human and divine futures, however, remain alethically settled. Even if God is not aware of those truths, they do not disappear. Instead, God becomes epistemically open to his future allowing him free and genuine loving responses to the creatures with whom he interacts. The problem of foreknowledge and freedom, therefore, can be dismissed by denying the traditional definition of omniscience as involving knowledge of the future. Such truths are not accessible to God by his own sovereign choice.

Involuntary Nescience

The next Open Theist view is Involuntary Nescience. Like Voluntary Nescience, Involuntary Nescience agrees that the future is alethically settled. As Richard Rice notes, even though God's foreknowledge may not be the cause of what happens, it is still true that something causes this knowledge such that God can know it. In order to avoid the determinism that follows from God's knowledge, Rice supports the idea that God can only know that which it is logically possible to know. Rice contends that it is not possible to know the future because of free will. As a result, God cannot be expected to know

---

18 John Tal Murphree, *Divine Paradoxes* (Christian Publications, 1998), 49–52. Murphree sees this position as being applicable only to a temporal God, a position he does not endorse.

something which is not possible to know. No one can do what is logically impossible. Rice contends that this position does not hold that God is limited or can be limited in his knowledge; therefore, it does not violate the concept of divine perfection.[19] God still perfectly knows all that it is possible to know.

William Hasker, the most prominent advocate of Involuntary Nescience, states that divine omniscience neither affirms nor presupposes that there are truths that exist yet logically cannot be known. All theists, however, should be willing to accept the fact that God can only know what it is logically possible to know.[20] At any time, God knows all propositions such that God's knowing them at that time is logically possible. Still, there may be propositions that are true, but God cannot logically know them. Hasker points specifically to truths about free agents. If actions are free in the libertarian sense, then it is not logically possible that God know them beforehand.[21] Hasker argues that God could have created a world that he controls in every detail and completely foreknows, but God did not believe such a world to be desirable. Instead, God created an open world where he is not in complete control. Hasker concludes that God cannot plan based on any *a priori* knowledge of how agents will respond or act because such knowledge does not technically exist.[22] Hasker is here endorsing Pike's argument concerning foreknowledge and freedom and rejects foreknowledge in order to dismiss the problem between the two.

Hasker defines his theory of divine omniscience according to the following principle:

> DO: God is omniscient=df. It is impossible that God should at any time believe what is false or fail to know any true proposition such that his knowing that proposition at that time is logically possible.

God cannot believe what is false and can only know what is logically possible to know. God's knowledge of the future includes all possible states of affairs, the likelihood of their outcomes, and those things that will necessarily exist. His foreknowledge of future contingents, however, is not known with certainty, only with probability. God knows himself, his purposes, and how best to carry them out. He knows all of the past and the present. He knows all

---

19 Richard Rice, "Divine Foreknowledge and Free Will," in *The Grace of God*, ed. Pinnock, 127–129.

20 William Hasker, *God, Time, and Knowledge* (Cornell University Press, 1989), 74. See also Richard Swinburne, *The Christian God* (Oxford, 1994), 131–33, Swinburne, *Coherence*, rev. ed., 175, and John Sanders, *The God Who Risks* (InterVarsity, 1998), 194.

21 William Hasker, "A Philosophical Perspective," in *The Openness of God*, ed. Clark Pinnock, et al. (InterVarsity Press, 1994), 136, 148.

22 Ibid., 151.

entities in the fullest measure, and everything God does is informed by this knowledge. He may know that allowing natural processes to continue unimpeded will be best, or he may know that his direct intervention, such as the miraculous, is required.[23] Hasker also argues that God can determine things by making offers to human agents that they cannot refuse based upon their inherent tendencies and dispositions. Hasker contends that this determinism is not manipulative since the agent is acting in accord with his own dispositions.[24] He argues elsewhere for a cautious libertarianism where most agent choices are made as a result of one's character, but this character is a formation of the free choices of the individual such that one maintains responsibility. Still, Hasker believes that there are many more chances for libertarian choices than this view implies. One may be determined to eat tomorrow, but one has the choice of what, when, and where to eat.[25]

When it comes to God's freedom, Hasker states that God must possess libertarian freedom. If he does not, then God must create out of the necessity of his nature making all of his actions necessary. Hasker believes that all theists accept this position. They all agree that God has choices, one of which is whether or not to create beings with libertarian freedom. If God does create such beings, then God will not have exhaustive knowledge of the future. If God does not create such beings, then God can know the future only at the price of human freedom.[26] Not wishing to deny the divine nature, Hasker argues that God is maximally intrinsically good but that he cannot be maximal in his productive goodness. According to Hasker, there is no maximal productive goodness for God. He could always do better. God could never exhaust his power to create something better than what he has created. As a result, there is no possible world that is sufficient to the measure of God's creative powers.[27]

From this conclusion, Hasker contends that God is not obligated to choose the best possible world. Hasker contends that there is no such world because values are not additive. Some competing goods are incommensurate with each other. They cannot be summed so as to make one world better than the other; therefore, God does not need to create at all. God is not necessitated to

---

23 Hasker, *God, Time, and Knowledge*, 187–188, 192.
24 Ibid., 194–196.
25 David Ciocchi, "The Religious Adequacy of Free-Will Theism," *RS* 38 (2002): 57; William Hasker, "Free Will Theism: A Reply to Ciocchi," *RS* 39 (2003): 437.
26 William Hasker, *Providence, Evil, and the Openness of God* (Routledge, 2004), 126–127.
27 Ibid., 176. The best possible world argument appears to imply the concept of marginal utility where an agent decides the increased or decreased value of one more unit. This valuation is subjective to the individual. As a result, there is no objective valuation to which God must adhere. It is only his opinion.

create nor does his life require creating in order to make it more wonderful.[28] Hasker concludes that creation cannot be explained by some necessity in the divine nature, by some lack in the divine nature, or by some superabundance that needs an outlet. God's act of creation is completely contingent and exists from grace; therefore, the divine nature cannot restrict divine freedom because God would be captive to his nature. Instead, Hasker maintains that the world is a free creation and has no explanation that shows why the world is the way that it is.[29] God is free from the bounds of nature and reason to act as he will; however, God will not do anything self-contradictory or in opposition to his perfect nature.[30]

For Involuntary Nescience, the future is alethically settled, but it is not logically possible for God to know those truths. The future, therefore, is epistemically open. These truths are separated from God and his knowledge unless he acquires them through the viewing of the temporal process. Both God and humans can be free because of God's inability to know those truths. Further, God can enjoy freedom since there is nothing within the divine nature that necessitates God choosing one way or the other. Even so, God will ultimately be consistent with his nature. Thus, the problem of foreknowledge and freedom is bypassed.

Non-Bivalent Omniscience

Other Open Theist positions reject the notion that the future is alethically settled. Non-Bivalent Omniscience holds that while the past and the present are real the future is non-existent. The contingent future only consists of certain trends and tendencies in the present that have not yet been fulfilled. As Peter Geach states, what "the Moving Finger has writ cannot be erased, but ahead of where it has written, there is only blank paper."[31] If this claim is correct, then the contingent future cannot be alethically settled. It must be open in its truth value. The principle of bivalence, therefore, which holds that a proposition must be either true or false cannot be correct.

In support of this idea, J. R. Lucas argues that the ordinary use of the word *know* does not in any way dictate certain knowledge. In fact, all it can dictate

---

28 Ibid., 179–183. See also Robert Adams, "Must God Create the Best?" in *The Virtue of Faith* (Oxford University Press, 1987), 55–57, and Mark Thomas, "Robert Adams and the Best Possible World," *FP* 13 (1996): 252–259.

29 Ibid., 184–85.

30 Hasker, "God Takes Risks," in *Contemporary Debates in Philosophy of Religion*, ed. Peterson and VanArragon, 220–221. This view appears to imply that God's perfect goodness is only accidental to his being rather than essential.

31 Peter Geach, *Providence and Evil* (Cambridge University Press, 1977), 52–53.

is probable knowledge; therefore, omniscience can only mean knowing what can be known, and the contingent future is not there to be known. Up until an event takes place, the event cannot be known since it is not real. As a result, future tense propositions about contingent events cannot be known prior to the event. A future tense proposition is made true by the actualizing of the events the proposition expresses.[32] Lucas further argues that knowledge of the contingent future would curtail divine freedom and omnipotence; therefore, such knowledge should be abandoned. God only knows what is possible to be known. If something cannot be done or known, then it is no derogation on the part of the agent that he cannot do it or know it.[33] As a result, it cannot be held against God's omniscience that knowledge of the contingent future is impossible to be known.

How then is the future not there to be truly known? As Dale Tuggy argues, libertarian freedom logically requires an open future and the unconditioned ability to act in more than one way.[34] He argues that time branches due to the reality of possibilities and the claim that all future possibilities are grounded in present conditions. Such possibilities are present facts about potentialities, which can be changed or annihilated. As a result, Tuggy believes that one can talk only about possible and impossible branches of the tree of possibilities. There is no actual world with a definite future because everything is constantly in flux. There is only an actual world with a possible future. If God has libertarian freedom essentially, he necessarily exists, and time does not end, then at no time is a complete world actual. Any contingent state of affairs may occur. Since there could never be a complete actual world, the concept of God picking a possible world to actualize unilaterally and completely is false. According to Tuggy, there can be some aspects of the future that will be definite, but the future is gappy. There is no complete future world segment or branch, only a partial segment with gaps to be filled. Only some propositions about the future are true or false, but not all. According to Tuggy, a proposition about the future can be true or false only if the event indicated by the proposition does or does not appear on all world branches. If the event appears or does not appear on all branches, then it has a truth value. If the event appears on some branches and not others, then it cannot be given a

---

32 J. R. Lucas, "Foreknowledge and the Vulnerability of God," in *The Philosophy in Christianity*, ed. Godfrey Vesey (Cambridge University Press, 1989), 120–124; J. R. Lucas, *The Future* (Basil Blackwell, 1989), 48, 221–222. See also William Hasker, *The Triumph of God Over Evil* (InterVarsity Press, 2008), 27–29.

33 Lucas, "Foreknowledge," 126; Lucas, *The Future*, 54, 226. The implication is that God is free and omnipotent. Since foreknowledge is incompatible with these things, foreknowledge must be impossible to possess.

34 Dale Tuggy, "Three Roads to Open Theism," *FP* 24 (2007): 32.

truth value.³⁵ Thus, bivalence must be denied of most propositions about the future since there is no future state to which such propositions correspond.

Tuggy argues that bivalent propositions about the future assume that some state of affairs must happen down the road. If something must definitely happen or not happen, those truths must take place. Either *p* definitely happens or definitely does not happen, or it is false that it is definite that *p* will happen or false that it is definite that *p* will not happen. Any way it is sliced, these are truths about the future that exist in the present and must take place. Tuggy also asserts that there are two different tenses regarding statements about the future. The simple future claims that at some future time an event will happen. The posterior present claims that as of today, something will definitely happen. Tuggy claims that posterior present statements do not run afoul of bivalence because they are false. Simple future statements cannot be either true or false since nothing in reality guarantees that they will or will not happen. Bivalence omniscience can block statements about the posterior present but not the simple future. Simple future statements will have to have a truth value if bivalence is upheld endangering indeterminacy.³⁶ Consequently, bivalence must be rejected. Deniers of bivalence will also reject the claim that all tenseless statements are true since this implies that an actual world exists and the branching model of time is false. They also deny that to assert that a proposition is not true is to assert its falsity and that to assert that a proposition is not false is to assert that it is true.³⁷

To escape the problem of foreknowledge and freedom, Non-Bivalent Omniscience holds that the future is not alethically settled. If the future is alethically settled, then claims about the future are either true or false. If they are true, then the events or actions specified by the claim must occur. Since the necessary occurrence of an action is inimical to freedom, bivalence must be rejected. Some claims about the future, particularly those concerning free action, do not possess a truth value. They do not possess a truth value because there is no future actually existing to which the claim may correspond. As a result, portions of the future are not settled but open. In fact, no possible world is actually complete. Any possible world is open to being actual at a given moment due to the actions of free agents; therefore, God does not know

---

35 Tuggy, "Three Roads to Open Theism," 33–34. J. R. Lucas and James Felt also agree with Tuggy concerning future truths being imbedded in present realities. See Lucas, *Freedom and Grace* (Eerdmans, 1976), 36–37; James Felt, "God's Choice: Reflections on Evil in a Created World," *FP* 1 (1984): 370–377.

36 Tuggy, "Three Roads to Open Theism," 35–39.

37 Ibid., 40–42. See also Richard Purtill, "Fatalism and the Omnitemporality of Truth," *FP* 5 (1988): 185–187.

those portions of the future that involve free agency, and freedom of the individual is preserved.

Bivalent Omniscience

Rejecting that the future is alethically settled, Bivalent Omniscience seeks a way to uphold that the future is alethically open while not violating the principle of bivalence: that every proposition has a truth value. Argued by figures such as Gregory Boyd and Alan Rhoda, this view posits the Incompatibility Thesis. This thesis is based on the argument that a semantically and metaphysically settled future is incompatible with future contingency. They argue that a semantically settled future implies a causally, or metaphysically, settled one. The word *will* has many uses. They emphasize that the predictive tense can be used both deterministically (if you drop the rock, it will fall) or indeterministcally (if you go out in the rain, you will catch a cold). The former implies definiteness while the latter implies probability. Boyd, Rhoda, and Belt also note that there are two different tense logics that can be used of the word *will*. The Ockhamist sense of *will* implies that the word *will* has no causal force at all. One is only predicting that something does happen and nothing more. The Peircean sense of *will* implies that the causal force of *will* is maximal. To say that something will happen is to say that it must causally happen. The Peircean sense says that *will* is incompatible with *might not*, affirming the Incompatibility Thesis. The Ockhamist sense implies that *will* is compatible with *might not*, denying the Incompatibility Thesis.[38]

Boyd, Rhoda, and Belt believe that the Peircean option better fits the standard usage of language. They argue that when people make predictions, they are either making a definitive claim or a probabilistic claim both of which imply causal connections and possibilities. People do often retroactively apply truth to *will*-statements that have happened; however, it does not follow that the statement was true when it was uttered. Also, any statement seems to imply a belief about something. Upon what is the belief of a *will*-statement based? If there is no reality on which to base the fact, then it cannot be true. It is only probable, not certain.[39]

---

38 Alan Rhoda, Gregory Boyd, and Thomas Belt, "Open Theism, Omniscience, and the Nature of the Future," *FP* 23 (2006): 438–439. For them, the use of the deterministic use of the word *will* implies that the laws of nature are deterministic. They may not be deterministic. Quantum mechanics seems to imply that the laws of nature, like the stone dropping, could fail to obtain.

39 Ibid., 442–446.

Assuming the correspondence theory of truth and an A theory of time, Boyd, Rhoda, and Belt argue for presentism. The view states that only the present actually exists, at least as it applies to future tensed statements. How then can a future tensed statement be true if there is no real future state of affairs to which it may correspond? For Boyd, Rhoda, and Belt, these statements must be grounded in present conditions. This grounding is only possible if the sufficient condition for a state of affairs already exists in the present, such as the natural laws regarding the sun's future rising; therefore, they claim that the Incompatibility Thesis is correct along with Peircean semantics.[40] Subsequently, they reject the claim that opposing future tensed statements whose truths are not grounded in present conditions are contradictories of each other as are their past and present tensed counterparts. The future is not fully determinate as the past and present are, so the claim does not hold. Boyd and Rhoda claim that contingent future tensed statements are contradicted by probability statements of what might or might not happen. Since they also do not wish to reject bivalence, Boyd and Rhoda argue that any contingent future tensed statement (even in its tenseless form) is false.[41]

Boyd asserts that this model of Open Theism is similar to the counterfactual statements of Molinism. According to Boyd, Molinists err in describing counterfactuals of freedom as what an agent would or will do. Rather, such counterfactuals should be described as what an agent might or might not do. Boyd believes that it is an ancient assumption that statements about the future must be contradictories. Instead, Boyd argues that the contradiction to "*x* would-will do *a* at *z*" is "*x* might not do *a* at *z*." The statement "*x* would-will not do *a* at *z*" is the contrary position, leaving *might* statements as sub-contraries. According to Boyd, *would*-counterfactuals do not exhaust the category of counterfactuals because there are three ontological positions: will, will not, and might or might not. God, therefore, must also know *might*-counterfactuals. He knows *would*-counterfactuals (will and will not) as false and *might*-counterfactuals as true. Boyd believes that it is impossible to know *would*-counterfactuals as true because that would imply knowing what a free being would do in a future state before that state is actualized. On the other hand, *would*-counterfactuals could be known as a result of God's will to create a world where the future is settled. *Would*-counterfactuals would stem either from a character that God gives an agent, making them not free, or from a character the agent acquires by free choice if they pursue possible actions. Since God created a world with *might*-counterfactuals, the future is open. As

---

40 Ibid., 446–448; Boyd, *God of the Possible*, 121–125.
41 Rhoda, Boyd, and Belt, "Open Theism," 450–454.

long as *might*-counterfactuals are true, there are no eternal facts, only eternal possibilities.[42]

Boyd believes that agents have some say in what occurs. Human beings can choose for or against God, but time slips away towards an inevitable conclusion where people will either be ensconced in their love for God or their rejection of God. As agent's act, they develop a character that limits their future choices; therefore, agents are moving from libertarian freedom to compatibilist freedom. Some become like Christ and love is their very being such that they can choose no other. Some are moving away from Christ into eternal rejection of him.[43]

Boyd also argues that God's nature is necessary. God must always be good, always love, and cannot change in his nature; however, Boyd argues that self-determining freedom still applies to God. The orthodox position holds that God possesses libertarian freedom; therefore, no necessity attaches to the divine choice forcing God to create or interact with his creation. Creating and interacting with creation are self-determining acts for God.[44] If God were like human agents, then he would not know his future. Any *would*-counterfactual concerning his future actions would be false since there is no reality or causal conditions to which those counterfactuals correspond. Instead, God could only know what he might or might not do, and this is true even though God is necessarily good and loving.

Bivalent Omniscience maintains that both God and human beings are free. The future is both epistemologically and alethically open. This claim is true because all future tensed statements about what will or would occur which are not grounded in present conditions are false. There can be no truth as to what a free agent will or would do since there is no reality to which these statements correspond. The only statements about the contingent future that can be true are those that state what might or might not occur allowing the future to be open. Both God and human beings, therefore, are free because

---

42 Boyd, *Satan and the Problem of Evil*, 126–28; Boyd, "God Limits His Control," 196–198, 198n29; idem, "An Open Theism Response (to William Lane Craig)," in *Divine Foreknowledge: Four Views* (InterVarsity Press, 2001), 144–148; idem, "Two Ancient (and Modern) Motivations for Ascribing Exhaustively Definite Foreknowledge to God: A Historic Overview and Critical Assessment," *RS* 46 (2010): 45–48. See also A. N. Prior, *Papers on Time and Tense* (Clarendon Press, 1968), 38–40, 58, 66–77. Boyd's final claim appears false. Possibilities are eternal facts because it is a fact that something is possible. Boyd appears to be asserting that there are no eternal facts about the future.

43 Boyd, "God Limits His Control," 192–195.

44 Boyd, *God of the Possible*, 136–37; idem, "Neo-Molinism and the Infinite Intelligence of God," *PC* 5 (2003): 193–94; idem, *Satan and the Problem of Evil*, 53–56, 69–70.

there is nothing that necessitates how they must act in the future. The future is unknowable.

Assessing the Theories

Having explicated the four Open Theist positions, determining which position is the best and which has the best chance of dismissing the problem of foreknowledge and divine freedom is pertinent. There are major problems with Voluntary Nescience that render it unsatisfactory. The first major problem is that the position appears to be incoherent on a number of levels. First, Avery Fouts argues that if God knew the future and then limited his awareness of it as Voluntary Nescience claims, the future is still settled and fixed in its truth. Forgetting or blocking the knowledge of these future truths does not undo the fixity of these truths. Not even backwards causation could undo them. Under Swinburne's position, Fouts claims that one must maintain that human actions necessarily happen in order to uphold the truths of the alethically settled future. Then, God's self-limitation of his knowledge suddenly changes these necessary and settled actions into possible and open actions.[45] This claim, however, is incoherent. If the action is alethically settled, then God cannot make that action contingent and open simply by becoming unaware of it. Further, God himself could never be free under Voluntary Nescience since all of his future actions are alethically settled, even the act of self-limitation.

Fouts further claims that if God is to preserve human and divine freedom, then God must have chosen to limit his knowledge from all eternity. If God had not chosen to self-limit himself from all eternity, then there would have been a time when God foreknew the future, denying the possibility of freedom for both himself and human beings. To preserve freedom, God could never at any time choose to become unaware of the future. He must have always chosen to be limited. If God must have always chosen to be limited, then God's choice to limit himself and possess freedom appears to be necessary and not free.[46]

Secondly, Fouts claims that Swinburne's argument makes divine freedom an accidental quality rather than a necessary one. This claim follows because Swinburne bases the existence of divine freedom in divine choice. If God were necessarily free, then he would not possess the power to self-limit. Such

---

45 Avery Fouts, "Divine Self-Limitation in Swinburne's Doctrine of Omniscience," *RS* 29 (1993): 22–23.
46 Ibid., 24.

a power would be unnecessary since God would already not know the future. If God is necessarily free, then God could never foreknow the future in the first place. Swinburne, however, accepts divine foreknowing and the need for God to self-limit. Divine freedom, therefore, cannot be necessary on Swinburne's view. God can only be free by choosing to be unaware of the future; therefore, God possesses freedom only if he chooses to possess it. Freedom is not something that God necessarily possesses. He has it only if he chooses to have it.[47]

Thirdly, Fouts notes that Swinburne believes that an agent is free in that he will perform an action only if he has no rational reason for refraining from doing that action. If God has no rational reason to refrain from self-limitation, then he cannot refrain from self-limitation. As a result, God's self-limitation is a necessary action, not a free one. Lastly, Fouts notes that Swinburne's argument presupposes that God could actually at some point make himself know the future that he had forgotten. If God can limit his awareness of the future, then he could undo that limitation and know the future again. Freedom, however, would be expunged if he did. If God does limit his knowledge in order to provide freedom, then God could never undo that limitation. If God cannot undo his self-limitation, then he is not free. Overall, Voluntary Nescience's talk of divine freedom is nonsense Fouts claims because God has no choice either to know the future or not know the future.[48] If God could know the future, then both divine and human freedom do not exist. If God must necessarily choose to limit himself so as to preserve human freedom and can never undo that choice, then divine freedom does not exist. Therefore, the view is incoherent.

Richard Rice also rejects selected ignorance on the grounds that it implies that the future is knowable and determined since it is alethically settled. If the future is settled and fixed in its truth, it is hard to see how freedom is possible. Also, Voluntary Nescience denies that God has perfect knowledge since there are truths that God does not know and could know. Plus, the view raises difficult questions. Does God eliminate his knowledge? Was God's knowledge exhaustive at one time but now not? How much can God forget? Can he remember that he forgot? Would such remembrance not imply that he knows what he forgot?[49] These same critiques apply to both Willard's and Murphree's views. It does not matter if God chooses never to think all truths or exercise all of his epistemic powers. The future is still settled, and libertar-

---

47 Ibid., 24–25.
48 Ibid., 25–26; Swinburne, *Coherence*, 148, 159, 269. See specifically Criterion A, B, and D.
49 Richard Rice, *God's Foreknowledge and Man's Free Will* (Bethany House Publishers, 1985), 31–32.

The Open Solution

ian freedom is not possible for either God or human beings. Thus, Voluntary Nescience does not imply an open future as the position claims.

Involuntary Nescience is susceptible to the same criticisms regarding the settled nature of the future that are applied to Voluntary Nescience. Both views regard the future as alethically settled; however, this settled future cannot be epistemically known. According to Involuntary Nescience, it is not logically possible for the contingent future to be epistemically known. If the future is alethically settled but not known by God, then the future is still fixed in its truth since it is alethically settled prior to the existence of future events. Consequently, all of God's choices are settled and fixed prior to those choices. He simply is unaware that they are settled and fixed. Merely being unaware of the future does not negate the fact that it is still settled and fixed in its truth value. If the future is settled and fixed, then there is no freedom for God or human beings according to Involuntary Nescience. Since these claims about the future are alethically settled, future events and actions cannot be other than what these claims state; therefore, libertarian freedom is denied.

Alan Rhoda notes two more problems with Involuntary Nescience. First, the proponent of Involuntary Nescience must explain why it is not logically possible to know alethically settled propositions about the future. These propositions cannot be unknowable because of their truth value, so something else makes them logically impossible for God or anyone else to know. What does this? There is no ready answer to this question. Second, Rhoda notes that Involuntary Nescience must reject the correspondence theory of truth since these alethically settled propositions about future contingent actions do not correspond to anything in reality. If there is no reality to which these propositions correspond, then such propositions are impossible to know because they would not be true.[50] Involuntary Nescience, however, holds that these propositions are true even though they do not correspond to any reality; therefore, it is not clear how these propositions can be alethically settled.

Finally, if the future is alethically settled, an aspect of reality seems necessary to direct both God and human beings to act in accordance with those settled truths even if no one can be aware of them. Both God and human beings seem to have a natural disposition to follow these truths blindly. Agents of any kind do not have the option of refraining from any action that is alethically settled; therefore, Involuntary Nescience does not seem to allow for the future to be open and for agents to be free in the libertarian sense.

---

50 Rhoda, "Generic Open Theism," 230.

Non-Bivalent Omniscience also has problems that do not make it an attractive Open Theist position. William Lane Craig argues that Non-Bivalent Omniscience misunderstands the correspondence theory of truth. According to Craig, to say that a statement corresponds to something does not mean that what it corresponds to must now exist. This notion is the opposite of what non-bivalent proponents say. They say the future cannot have truth values since the future does not exist. Statements about the future do not correspond to anything. Craig claims that the same claims would also be true of the past. The past does not literally exist; therefore, statements about the past cannot correspond to the past. People, however, can still make truth claims about the past. As long as the events existed, such statements can be made. Analogously, future statements can be true based on the claim that the events they indicate will exist. All that is required is that when the moment arrives, the statement will be upheld to be true.[51] Craig goes on to claim that the same facts ground the truth of both past, present, and future tense statements. *It will rain tomorrow* and *it rained yesterday* are both true because they point to the same day and event. Events guarantee that a future tensed statement is true before the events occur. If future tensed statements have no truth because they do not exist, then past statements cannot have truth since they do not exist.[52] Since proponents of Non-Bivalent Omniscience hold to the correspondence of truth claims with the past, they can also hold to the correspondence of truth claims with the future; therefore, there is little reason to reject bivalence.

Even if one rejects Craig's definition of the correspondence theory of truth, there is still an issue that arises with this theory. This theory of truth requires that a truth claim possesses or did possess a correspondence relation with reality. If no correspondence relation exits or did exist, then the claim cannot be true and must be false. As a result, there seems to be no room for a neutral position regarding the truth of proposition. Propositions either have a correspondence relation with some sort of reality or do not; therefore, they are either true or false, not neutral. It is difficult to see how the correspondence theory of truth can be accepted and bivalence can be rejected. Perhaps the proponent of Non-Bivalent Omniscience could accept a different theory of truth, but then it becomes questionable if the Non-Bivalent position remains tenable in its current form.

---

51 William Lane Craig, "What Does God Know?" in *God Under Fire*, ed. Douglas Huffman and Eric Johnson (Zondervan, 2002), 144; idem, *The Only Wise God* (Wipf and Stock, 1999), 55–57. See also Charles Bayliss, "Are Some Propositions Neither True Nor False?" *POS* 3 (1936): 156–166, on how correspondence theory works concerning future-tensed propositions.

52 Craig, "What Does God Know?" 145; idem, *Only Wise God*, 58–59.

The Open Solution

Craig notes a second problem for Non-Bivalent Omniscience. If there are no truth values for propositions about the future, then a future tensed statement that is a compound of two *will* or *will not* statements cannot be true. Statements such as, "Hillary Clinton will or will not win the presidential election in 2016" cannot have truth value if bivalence is rejected. Since neither simple statement has a truth value, then the compound statement cannot as well. This conclusion, however, seems absurd since either Clinton will or will not win. The logical structure of the claim seems to imply that it has a truth value. There is no other alternative. Also, truth cannot be applied to the statement "Hillary Clinton will both win and not win the presidential election of 2016." This statement is clearly false since it involves a contradiction. One cannot both win and not win at the same time.[53] The same could be said of statements such as "God will and will not do *A*." Non-Bivalent Omniscience thus leads to absurdities and contradictions with its rejection of bivalent propositional truth values.

As a result, Bivalent Omniscience is the only position that remains as a viable candidate for dismissing the problem of foreknowledge and divine freedom. Bivalent Omniscience does not succumb to the criticism that the actions of all agents are alethically settled and therefore not free since this position rejects an alethically settled future. The future is open since the only alethically settled truths are about what might or might not happen. Thus, no agent is necessitated to perform a specific action at a specific time. Bivalent Omniscience also does not imply that there are truths that God could fail to know either by self-limitation or impossibility. God is fully aware at all times of what is true; therefore, this position maintains a robust conception of divine omniscience. Lastly, Bivalent Omniscience does not succumb to the absurdities of rejecting bivalence. All propositions have a truth claim.

As a result, Bivalent Omniscience could also apply to God and his situation. Most claims concerning God's specific future actions are false. General claims, such as "God will not lie," are true since they necessarily flow from the perfectly good divine nature, but specific claims, such as "God will do *x*," are false if they do not necessarily flow from any aspect of the divine nature. True statements that can be made about God's specific future actions are those that pertain to what God might or might not do. As a result, God's future is open rather than fixed. There is a plethora of things that God might do but no specific thing that he must do; therefore, God is made free by rejecting

---

53 Craig, "What Does God Know?," 145–146; Craig, *Only Wise God*, 59–63; Rhoda, "Generic Open Theism," 230–231; A. N. Prior, *Past, Present, and Future* (Oxford University Press, 1967), 135.

the claim that God can know the contingent future, and the problem of foreknowledge and divine freedom is dismissed.

Divine Freedom and Bivalent Omniscience

I have concluded that Bivalent Omniscience is the best Open Theist position and is a candidate for dismissing the problem of foreknowledge and divine freedom. Does this position succeed? The first major problem with Bivalent Omniscience is that it requires a rejection of the theory of divine ideas. I argued in chapter one that God knows exactly how he will act in any possible world he chooses to create via the divine ideas. Since possible worlds exist as forms in the divine mind, God knows the entire temporal history of every possible world and all events and actions that they contain, such as God's parting of the Red Sea. As a result, God knows precisely how he will choose and act within any possible world that he chooses to create since that world will unfold according to the divine idea; therefore, God is necessitated to act according to the dictates of his divine idea he actualizes. For God to do otherwise would be irrational and less than perfectly good neither of which is possible for God. God must, therefore, either be a compatibilist in those choices or have no freedom at all. The same conclusion applies to Christ who exists and acts within the world.[54] As a result, future tensed contingent propositions regarding the divine future do not appear to be false. The theory of divine ideas suggests that they can be true and that God is naturally necessitated to obey the dictates of his divine ideas that he actualizes. Since the theory of divine ideas is assumed as the correct understanding of the grounds of God's omniscience, how Bivalent Omniscience can overcome this problem without rejecting the theory is difficult to see.

A second set of problems for the Bivalent Omniscience position is evident from Boyd's claim concerning freedom and the divine nature. First, Boyd claims that the divine nature, even Christ's nature, of goodness and love is necessary. The Godhead cannot act in conflict with this nature; otherwise, the Trinity would be less that perfectly good. No person of the Trinity is able to acquire this character as Boyd asserts that human beings can; therefore, the divine nature has a determining and necessitating effect on the divine choices. Any divine choice determined by the divine nature must be either logically or naturally necessitated and cannot be libertarianly free.

---

54 See William Lane Craig, "Response to Gregory A. Boyd," in *Four Views on Divine Providence*, ed. Stanley Gundry (Zondervan, 2011), 225; Gregory Boyd, "Christian Love and Academic Dialog: a Reply to Bruce Ware," *JETS* 45 (2002): 242.

Second, Boyd contends that for a human being to be like Christ requires the movement from libertarian to compatibilist freedom. Since Christ acts in accordance with the dictates of the divine nature, human agents must develop a character like Christ's that is ensconced in love. If this claim is true, then it follows that Christ, the Divine Son, has compatibilist freedom, not libertarian freedom. If Christ is a compatibilist and Christ is God, then God appears to be a compatibilist and not a libertarian in his freedom. As a result, the divine Godhead would be determined by the divine nature and is naturally necessitated. Such an implication is contradictory to the Open Theist enterprise for Open Theism requires the truth of libertarian freedom. It rejects any other definition. Further, this implication is contrary to Boyd's own claims that God has libertarian freedom. Boyd, therefore, appears to be mistaken in his claim that being like Christ requires agents to have compatibilist freedom. Boyd must reject the possibility that the divine nature determines the divine choice for his theory to work.

Can this claim be rejected? That God finds himself in a situation in which he has only one morally good option available seems possible. Such possibility is demonstrated by the theory of divine ideas. If the theory of divine ideas is correct, then all of the divine choices save the choice to create are situations in which God has only one morally good option available; therefore, God would be naturally necessitated in those choices. God appears to have self-determining freedom in only one instance at best: the instance of creation. The rest of the divine life is not free. These implications also undermine the central claim of the Bivalent Omniscience position that all *would*-counterfactuals are false because the implications of the divine nature and the divine ideas can make some of them true. Again, Bivalent Omniscience does not appear able to deliver God from the clutches of natural necessity.

Another problem revolves around how propositions possess their truth value. Bivalent Omniscience asserts that propositions about future contingents are false, and God knows them as false. When God makes his choice of what to will, could he then change their truth value? This concept is not the same as making a proposition true. An agent can make a proposition true but not change the proposition's truth value. Does God have the power to change a proposition's truth value and thus to change his omniscient knowledge? If such a power exists, then God could change the truth value of any *would*-counterfactual, even those about himself. Consequently, future contingent propositions are not necessarily false. They could be true. Further, God could know the future, including his own future, by changing the truth value of future contingent propositions. Such a change would make him unfree.

Unless such a power can be shown to be illogical, God could know propositions about the future, even his own, as true should he so choose to determine the future. If God can and does determine his own future and libertarian freedom is the only viable form of freedom, then how is God free regarding those determined choices? The onus is on the proponent of Bivalent Omniscience to demonstrate that God does not have such a power to change truth values.

According to William Lane Craig, a fourth problem for Bivalent Omniscience is that in counterfactual discourse the word *might* is opposed by the word *would*, not *will*. The terms *will* and *would* do not have the same meaning. For example, the sentence *I would eat pizza for lunch* indicates that I cannot fail to eat pizza for lunch. On the other hand, the sentence *I will eat pizza for lunch* does not indicate that I cannot fail to eat pizza for lunch. It only indicates that an action occurs at a later time. It remains possible that I not eat pizza for lunch or that I eat something else for lunch; therefore, the terms *would* and *will* cannot be used interchangeably. On the other hand, the terms *might* and *will* are interchangeable. *Might* is a modal locution, but *will* is a non-modal locution. *Will* is just the future tense of a verb. One can express that something will occur but might not occur, which is just to portend that the event is contingent. This notion was expressed in the sentence *I will eat pizza for lunch*. The event will occur but logically might not occur. Craig claims that proponents of Bivalent Omniscience have misused English in their definition of *might* and *will* propositions. As a result, Craig argues that Bivalent Omniscience has created a false opposition with its *might* and *would*-counterfactuals due to this confusion. He claims that one can make true statements about both what might happen and what will happen, and there is no contradictory between them. Craig argues that proponents of Bivalent Omniscience must believe that *will*-propositions are disguised modal statements, such as *must*-propositions, for their view to work.[55] The proponent of Bivalent Omniscience, however, could simply abandon the term *will* in favor of *would* and keep his argument intact, or he could insist that the term *will* does convey a modal locution, like *must*.

Does the Bivalent Omniscience position regarding the claim that *would*-counterfactuals are contraries with each other succeed? Contraries cannot both be true; yet, they can both be false. As a result, "*x* would do *a* at *z*" and "*x* would not do *a* at *z*" can both be false. These two false statements, however, do not necessarily appear to be contraries. If "*x* would do *a* at *z*" is

---

[55] Craig, "Response to Gregory A. Boyd," 227–229. Recent discussion on this issue has both critiqued and defended Craig's claims. See Elijah Hess, "Arguing from Molinism to Neo-Molinism," *PC* 17, no. 2 (2015): 331–351, and Kirk MacGregor, "The Neo-Molinist Square Collapses: A Molinist Response to Elijah Hess," *PC* 18, no. 1 (2016): 195–206.

false, then it is implied that "x would not do a at z" is true, and if "x would not do a at z" is false, then it is implied that "x would do a at z" is true. They cannot both be false; however, they also cannot both be true since it is contradictory to say that x both would and would not do a at z. It is impossible for X to both do and refrain from doing a at z. As a result, such counterfactuals would actually be contradictories, not contraries as Bivalent Omniscience asserts. They both cannot be true and both cannot be false. One of these *would*-counterfactuals must be true and must be knowable by God. If this is the case, why then should one accept Rhoda's and Boyd's position as correct?

Further, there is reason to believe that there are true *would*-counterfactuals given the theory of divine ideas and the perfectly good nature of God. Since God can only do that which is good and rational, there will be true and false *would*-counterfactuals concerning God in some circumstance that he might encounter. For example, there would be situations in which God only has one good or rational option. The theory of divine ideas implies such a possibility with its dictates on divine actions in actualized possible worlds. Rhoda's and Boyd's claim can also be called into question if God possesses the power to change the truth value of *would*-counterfactuals. If God can change these truth values, then these counterfactuals are no longer contraries since it is impossible for an agent to both do and refrain from doing an action at the same time. How then can Rhoda and Boyd claim that *would*-counterfactuals are contraries and cannot be true? Rhoda and Boyd have failed to prove their claim; therefore, God's future choices and actions are still determined and knowable making him unfree.

Finally, there is good theological evidence to question the legitimacy of Bivalent Omniscience. In Isa 41:21–24, God challenges the idols of the nation to demonstrate that they are divine. One of the challenges that God issues them is to reveal the future. God here states that the ability to know and declare the future is a mark of divinity; however, the Open View denies that God has such knowledge and the ability to declare the future. According to Bivalent Omniscience, everything God knows about the future is literally false and not something God can declare will or would occur. In other words, God fails his own test for divinity. He cannot declare the future and prove his own divinity. He is no better than the idols, which God calls "nothing." This implication is a serious problem for Bivalent Omniscience for it demeans both the biblical witness and God himself.

Further, the implications of Bivalent Omniscience indicate that God is incapable of making a promise or declaration of future action. Since God does not know the future due to free will, God cannot declare what he will do at some later point in time because he cannot guarantee that he will be able to do it. For example, God cannot declare through Jeremiah that he will bring Babylon against Israel in judgment. Due to free will, God cannot guarantee that Babylon will be enticed to come against Israel. He cannot even guarantee that Babylon will continue to be in existence such that they can be his tool of judgment. The free choices of human agents could thwart his plans and reduce his claim to falsehood. As a result, God cannot make promises or declarations of future actions; however, the Bible is replete with such promises and declarations. If Bivalent Omniscience is correct then those proclamations are literally false, and God has spoken a falsehood. Again, this implication is demeaning both to God and the biblical witness.

Conclusion

After surveying the Open Solution's contenders to dismiss the problem of foreknowledge and divine freedom dilemma, I concluded that the best position of the Open View is Bivalent Omniscience. Voluntary Nescience did not allow for an open future due to its support of an alethically settled future. The position only made the matter worse with its claim that God could willingly forget about his knowledge of that future. This claim led to implications that made the theory incoherent. Involuntary Nescience also did not allow for an open future since it also holds to the claim that the future is alethically settled. Simply because God logically cannot know that settled future does not negate the fact that the future is settled and necessitates God's action. Further, this position cannot explain why it is logically impossible that either God or any other agent know the future. Lastly, Non-Bivalent Omniscience fails because it suffers from logical absurdities that render it unacceptable.

Even though Bivalent Omniscience was determined to be the best version of the Open View and the most viable candidate for dismissing the problem of foreknowledge and divine freedom, several troubling issues were found with the position. The position could not incorporate the theory of divine ideas in a manner that did not negatively affect the divine freedom. As a result, God became subject to natural necessity in the majority of his choices. This implication also demonstrates that the claims of Bivalent Omniscience are false. Contingent propositions about the future can be true and known. This position also cannot demonstrate that it is logically impossible that God should somehow find himself in a situation where he has only one morally good option available. Since such a state of affairs is possible, Bivalent Omniscience cannot demonstrate that God is never necessitated by his nature.

Also, the logical system the Bivalent Omniscience utilizes does not appear to be correct. Lastly, Bivalent Omniscience is not in accord with the biblical witness when it comes to the nature of God or his ability to declare his future intentions.

As a result of these criticisms, I conclude that the Open Solution fails to dismiss the problem of foreknowledge and divine freedom. Bivalent Omniscience violates the criteria of avoiding the implication that God acts by natural necessity. The position also violates the criteria to incorporate the theory of divine ideas in a manner that allows for divine freedom. As a result, I reject the Open Solution as a successful attempt to dismiss the problem of foreknowledge and divine freedom.

CHAPTER 4

THE MOLINIST SOLUTION

In chapter three, the Open Solution was considered as a potential means to dismiss the problem of foreknowledge and divine freedom. This position argues that the future is open to possibility rather than being closed and knowable by God. Ultimately, the Open Solution was rejected as a viable resolution for the problem of foreknowledge and divine freedom. It still seems possible that the divine future can be closed and known. A satisfactory solution to the problem of foreknowledge and divine freedom will require a position that allows for God to know his future yet remain free. As a result, I will now turn to an examination of a theory that would allow for a future that is closed and knowable, yet free.

The position to be examined in this chapter is called the Molinist Solution. Molinism appeals to what are called counterfactuals of creaturely freedom as the means by which God arranges and knows the future while maintaining human freedom. This mechanism could be used to understand how God knows his own future while remaining free. In the first section, I discuss the Molinist position. I then examine the different variations for understanding how counterfactuals of creaturely freedom are known by God. I argue that there is only one available option for the Molinist. Thirdly, I apply the Molinist theory of counterfactuals of freedom to the divine situation. Finally, I explain why this solution fails to solve the problem of foreknowledge and divine freedom and should be rejected.

MOLINISM

The theory of Molinism was first developed by Luis de Molina. Molina disputes that Aquinas believed that God foreknows the future based solely on the divine ideas. He believes that Aquinas would have devoted more time to such an explanation rather than affirming timelessness as the solution. Molina, however, also argues that Aquinas would not swing entirely in the other direction either. He would affirm both timelessness and the theory of divine ideas.[1] But how could this be done? Molina argues that God knows the future because he knows what every agent would freely do in any circumstance. God then chooses to establish certain circumstances based on this knowledge of how agents would act. He establishes this order of circumstances freely by his own decree and knows it logically prior to the existence of anything either in time or in eternity.[2]

Molina argues that there are three types of divine knowledge. First, Molina holds that God knows all necessary and possible things with certainty. He knows them because he is the primary cause, and he knows them through his knowledge of the secondary causes (agents and objects) that bring them about. God knows all things that could take place due to this natural knowledge. This knowledge represents the things that God could decree and exists logically prior to his will. The second type of divine knowledge is God's free knowledge. This knowledge incorporates contingent things that exist because God wills them to exist. Because free knowledge encompasses everything that God has decreed to exist by his free will, God knows all future things determinately without condition. He knows what will occur as well as what will not occur.[3] The final type of divine knowledge is God's middle knowledge, which is situated conceptually between his natural and free knowledge. God knows how creaturely freedom would be used if that creature were placed in certain circumstances. Middle knowledge is similar to natural knowledge in that it is logically prior to God's free act of creation, and God did not have the power to know differently than he does. Middle Knowledge is similar to free knowledge in that it indicates the choices of free agents and could have been different from what it is. Its content could be opposite of what it is, and God would have known that if it had been so. Middle knowledge, however, is not determined by the divine will; therefore, middle knowledge is different than free

---

[1] Luis de Molina, *On Divine Foreknowledge: Part IV of the Concordia*, trans. Alfred Freddoso (Cornell University Press, 1988), 4.49.1–7.

[2] Ibid., 4.49.8. Molina rejects divine timelessness on the grounds that it implies that things exist in eternity prior to existing in time. Contingent things are not able to exist prior to their actual existence in time. Also, he believes it implies that an infinite number of things and events already exist in the eternal now since it has no beginning or end. See 4.49.16–20, 4.52.19. See also William Lane Craig, *The Problem of Divine Foreknowledge and Future Contingents from Aristotle to Suarez* (Brill, 1988), 171–172, 178; Alfred Freddoso, "Introduction," in Luis de Molina, *On Divine Foreknowledge*, 30–36.

[3] Molina, *On Divine Foreknowledge*, 4.50.16–17, 4.52.9.

knowledge because it exists logically prior to God's will and God is not able to affect it. It is also different than natural knowledge because God could have known differently in his middle knowledge since creatures could have done otherwise. If they had done otherwise, then God would have known that very thing. His middle knowledge is not necessary as his natural knowledge is.[4]

With this framework, Molina argues that an agent with free will does not act because of the divine foreknowledge or because of the divine will. Rather, the agent's action is foreknown because God knows that the agent would freely act a certain way. God foresees based on the understanding that in a certain situation the creature will freely act in a certain manner.[5] But how does God possess this knowledge? Molina rejects that free choices are determined by the nature of the agent. Agents exceed their nature and are not controlled by it, so God cannot know free choices by knowing the agent and his nature. The future of any agent, even God, is not based upon the divine nature.[6] Instead, Molina argues for a divine super-comprehension of all agents. God knows agents through his middle knowledge so well that he can know exactly how they would act in certain situations.

Molina argues, however, that God does not foreknow his own choices because he does not see himself within the same absolutely preeminent comprehension that he does creatures. God cannot see via his natural or middle knowledge what he would do because his intellect does not surpass the divine being. As a result, God cannot know himself in intricate detail so as to know how he would act. In the same way, the creature does not know himself intricately, for his knowledge does not surpass his own essence. Creatures cannot know how they would act just as God cannot know how he would act. Molina believes that if God knew what he would do, his freedom would be eliminated. If middle knowledge of divine counterfactuals of freedom would rob God of freedom, then why does middle knowledge not rob creatures of their freedom? Molina thinks that the difference is that human agents are ignorant of the truths of middle knowledge while God is not. God can know what agents would do without issue, but he cannot know what he would do without robbing himself of freedom. Instead, God knows how he would act after his free decision, so such knowledge is a part of his free knowledge.[7]

---

4 Ibid., 4.50.15, 4.52.9–10. See also William Lane Craig, *Divine Foreknowledge and Human Freedom* (Brill, 1991), 239–240; idem, *The Problem of Divine Foreknowledge*, 172–177.

5 Molina, *On Divine Foreknowledge*, 4.52.10.

6 Ibid., 4.52.14–17; Freddoso, "Introduction," 54.

7 Ibid., 4.52.11, 4.52.12. See also Craig, *Divine Foreknowledge and Human Freedom*, 238, 275–277, Craig, *The Problem of Divine Foreknowledge*, 179–81, and Freddoso, "Introduction," 52. Craig notes that Francisco Suarez argues that since middle knowledge is based on free will, then such knowledge of divine choices cannot be endangered since freedom is not removed by

The contemporary explanation of Molinism utilizes the same framework of knowledge as Molina and develops an implicit framework of logical moments. Logical priority is something serving to explain another thing. The explanatory thing is not temporally prior to the explained thing. These things could be temporally simultaneous. Logical priority is like logical arguments where the premises are logically prior to the conclusion but the truth of all statements is temporally simultaneous. Future events are temporally posterior to foreknowledge but logically prior to it. Whatever God knows, he knows from eternity so that there is no temporal succession in God's knowledge. Because of omniscience, he cannot be accused of lacking knowledge at any time. However, there is a logical succession in God knowing that certain propositions are conditionally or explanatorily prior to others. This succession has an asymmetrical dependence between propositions. In the first logical moment, God knows all that is possible through natural knowledge. In the second logical moment, God has middle knowledge of what the free creature would do in any circumstance rather than what the agent could do. Middle knowledge is only partially explained by natural knowledge in that middle knowledge involves logical possibilities. Natural knowledge, however, does not explain what the agent would do. The third logical moment is God's free choice. God's act is explained by his knowledge of what could and would occur. In the last logical moment, God has free knowledge of the reality he chooses to instantiate. This decision is the result of a complete and unlimited deliberation in which God weighs all options and settles on one particular world that he desires. This knowledge is also not essential to God.[8] This logical and conceptual framework helps explain how God utilizes middle knowledge in his creative choice.

Middle knowledge is thus a vital part of God's omniscience and providence. As Thomas Flint claims, God must also know counterfactuals of freedom about non-actual people as well as actual people; otherwise, God is restricted to creating only those people he knows will be actual. There would

---

these counterfactuals. So God can know what he would do in his middle knowledge. He knows this intuitively. See Craig, *Divine Foreknowledge and Human Freedom*, 239, 275–277; Craig, *The Problem of Divine Foreknowledge*, 225–226, 30–32; Eef Dekker, *Middle Knowledge* (Peeters, 2000), 102–103; Francisco Suarez, *Opera Omnia: De scientia Dei*, 2.7-8, ed. M. Andre and C. Brenton (Paris: Vivès, 1856–1878), and Francisco Suarez, *Opera Omnia: Opusculum*, 2-7, ed. M. Andre and C. Brenton (Paris: Vivès, 1856–1878). Molina's view also suggests that freedom amounts to ignorance, but this implication is questionable. An agent might be determined and unfree but not know that he is unfree; therefore, ignorance does not imply freedom.

8 Craig, *Divine Foreknowledge and Human Freedom*, 237–239; idem, *The Only Wise God* (Wipf and Stock, 1987), 127–131; Dekker, *Middle Knowledge*, 5–9; Thomas Flint, *Divine Providence* (Cornell University Press, 1998), 37, 42–44.

be no other possible persons. Further, the set of true counterfactuals limit the worlds that God could create. The set of counterfactual truths could be different resulting in different counterfactual situations. If a certain set of counterfactuals of freedom is true, then God must create according to that set of truths. God is logically restricted to creating those creaturely-world types that are compatible with the set of counterfactuals of freedom he knows as true.[9] These world types (worlds that correspond to the set of true counterfactuals of freedom) are contingently actual, and God has no control over which world type is actual. In fact, there are many worlds that God cannot actualize because they do not fall into the world type that is actual. Flint calls these world types a galaxy. Those worlds in the galaxy are feasible to be actualized while those that are not in the galaxy are infeasible. The same concept of feasibility can be extended to galaxies as well.[10] Since some galaxies are not actual, then those non-actual galaxies, along with their possible worlds, are not feasible for God to create. As a result, Alfred Freddoso claims that God finds himself in creation situations. A creation situation is where God is presented with all of the feasible options for creation, including entire possible worlds. God finds himself in this situation rather than creating the situation. This state is logically prior to God's volition, and it determines which objects of middle knowledge are true. Thus, there are many different creation situations, each with its own sets of truths and possible worlds. God then creates out of the possible worlds that are a part of the creation situation.[11]

Knowledge of Counterfactuals of Freedom

Molinism depends on the concept of middle knowledge and the existence of these counterfactuals of freedom, but how are these counterfactuals known? Contemporary Molinists propose many different theories on how God possesses that knowledge. Jonathan Kvanvig believes that God, in order to preserve the freedom of the creature, does not create an entire world. Rather, he creates part of a world and then allows free creatures to determine the manner in which that world unfolds. They do so according to the set of all possible outcomes for that world, which God knows. Kvanvig also holds that God actualizes essences but does not create them since essences are necessarily existent. These essences establish what an agent would freely do in any

---

9 Ibid., 47–48.
10 Ibid., 51.
11 Freddoso, "Introduction," 48; Dekker, *Middle Knowledge,* 9–12. Dekker notes that Banezians, the chief antagonists of Molina, argued that there is only one creation situation.

possible world, and this maximal subjunctive of freedom is contingent, not necessary.¹²

Instead of appealing to the nature of the agent for explaining how counterfactuals of freedom are known, Freddoso claims that a counterfactual of freedom can have grounds just in case at some point in the future there will be grounds for it. This argument is analogous to the claim that a past proposition is true in that there were grounds for it.¹³ As Flint explains, if one makes a claim that later turns out to be true, he can say that his previous statement was true because grounds now exist for that statement's truth. Even if the certainty of such a claim is questioned at the time it is made, this questioning only involves the epistemic probability of the claim and not metaphysical probability of the claim. The metaphysical facts are that the statement was believed true and what it refers to is true. Past-tensed propositions are grounded just in case the events they refer to did occur, making such a present-tensed proposition true. *Bill Clinton decided to run for president* is true and grounded just in case it is true that *Bill Clinton decides to run for president* is true and grounded. In other words, the claim "it was the case that z" is now grounded if and only if the claim "z is now grounded" was the case. This conception of grounding also applies to future statements. "It will be the case that z" is now grounded if and only if "z is now grounded" will be the case.¹⁴ As Craig asserts, such a view holds that the correspondence theory of truth does not require the ontological existence of the reality to which a propositions points.¹⁵ Counterfactual claims, such as "In circumstance c, agent a would freely choose x," can be true even though circumstance c and the agent's freely choosing x do not yet obtain.

Others, such as Eef Dekker, believe that counterfactual power over the past is essential to any theory of middle knowledge. Counterfactual power

---

12 Kvanvig, *Possibility of an All-Knowing God*, 121–126; Dekker, *Middle Knowledge*, 12–14.

13 Freddoso, "Introduction," 71–74; See also Flint, 129; Dekker, *Middle Knowledge*, 45; Kvanvig, *Possibility of an All-Knowing*, 136–137; Craig, *Divine Foreknowledge and Human Freedom*, 260; Richard Otte, "A Defense of Middle Knowledge," *IJPR* 21 (1987): 161–169. Freddoso's claim here has a flaw. There are counterfactuals of freedom that are never instantiated. Since there will be no grounds at any point for these counterfactuals, then they lack a ground for their truth. Therefore, any non-instantiated counterfactual of freedom cannot be true; however this is in conflict with the Molinist view which states that such true counterfactuals are true.

14 Flint, *Divine Providence*, 130–132. The same flaw in Freddoso's argument pointed out in the previous footnote applies here as well. What grounds future propositions, such as counterfactuals of freedom, which will not at any point have a ground? It seems that they lack truth even though they are part of the actual galaxy of feasible worlds.

15 Craig, *Only Wise God*, 56–58, 140. Craig's claim here is questionable. The correspondence theory of truth relies on a correspondence relation between a proposition and reality. It is this relation that establishes truth. If there is no such relation since there is no reality with which to correspond, then how can that proposition be true?

over the past is the ability to have acted differently such that the past would have been different. This results in a non-necessity of the past.[16] He argues that counterfactuals of freedom are not causally dependent on the agent's action because of this counterfactual freedom over the past. Agents bring about the truth of a counterfactual of freedom if and only if the circumstances obtain requiring the action specified. If the action does not occur, then the counterfactual is false. According to Dekker, the truth of counterfactuals of freedom is brought about in a non-causal way. Agents can act such that their actions bring about but do not cause certain consequences. For example, the jailor who gives Socrates hemlock brings about but does not cause the widowhood of Socrates' wife Xantippe. The widowhood of Xantippe is caused by Socrates' death. Dekker claims this concept applies to an agent's bringing about counterfactual truths. He believes that Molinists want causal independence rather than causal dependence between the agent and the counterfactual of freedom. He also claims that Molinists can hold to counterfactual dependency and logical priority at the same time. These two concepts do not necessarily run in the same direction.[17] Dekker argues for a synchronically contingent relation between causal antecedents and free choice. That is, it cannot be a free choice if the choice was determined by some events prior to the choice. Any causes that bring about a free choice are simultaneous with the free choice.[18] Thus, God concursively cooperates with human freedom. God's action is neither later than nor prior to the human choice but simultaneous with it. God does not cause the free action nor does the free action cause God's action.[19]

Other Molinists reject that all knowledge is based in sense perception or causal inference. The truth of counterfactuals of freedom is not determined by creatures for several reasons. First, such counterfactuals are true logically prior to the existence of agents. Second, some of these counterfactuals are about agents that do not exist. Third, because agents are caused to exist by God, they cannot ground his middle knowledge. Fourth, an agent's character

---

16 Dekker, *Middle Knowledge*, 21–22, 77. See also Eef Dekker, "Explanatory Priority and Independence: On an Argument against Middle Knowledge," *Sophia* 38 (1999): 3–4, 9.

17 Dekker, *Middle Knowledge*, 65–71.

18 Ibid., 111. Dekker goes on to state that rather than being unfree because of their character, agents always have the metaphysical power to act opposite their moral inclinations; however, one would rarely, if ever, go against them. Agents can still be ultimately responsible for unfree acts if they are the ultimate source of their character. This presents a layered aspect to freedom. Formal freedom is the reality that one can do otherwise while material freedom is controlled by the beliefs and character that one develops as he acts. The former is always open and free while the latter can be completely unfree. So the agent always possesses the power to do otherwise even if he cannot or rarely can exercise it. See ibid., 114–118.

19 Ibid., 119–120, 123.

is a product of his choices making it an improper ground. Counterfactuals of freedom also are not grounded in God's will or the actual choices of human agents. Instead, no one and nothing grounds their truth.[20] Consequently, Craig argues for a rational or conceptualist model of omniscience where God innately knows future-tensed statements. As a result, God can have knowledge of future-tensed statements in two ways. First, it could be innate and logically foundational. Like a brute fact, this knowledge of true future-tensed statements is something that God just possesses. Second, this knowledge of future-tensed statements could be based on true or false statements that are logically prior to that knowledge and enable him to know the truth of these future-tensed statements. Craig notes that this is like middle knowledge, where God's knowledge of the future is based on his logically prior knowledge of counterfactuals of freedom. Given the possibility of this conceptualist model, any perceptual model should be discarded, Craig claims. God never learns of counterfactuals of freedom because he has always innately known them. There is no explanation for the truth of these counterfactuals and how they are grounded; therefore, one need not ask for an explanation, Craig claims.[21] Counterfactuals of freedom possessing the truth value that they have and God knowing them are just brute facts.

Choosing a Method of Knowing

If God possesses middle knowledge, how does God know of these counterfactuals of freedom? Kvanvig's method was to ground counterfactuals of freedom in the nature and character of an agent. Kvanvig's approach, however, violates Molina's insistence that counterfactuals of freedom are not grounded in the essence or nature of agents. It would deny libertarian freedom. The reason that grounding counterfactual knowledge in an agent's nature denies libertarian freedom is because on this view the agent's action necessarily flows from the agent's nature. Thus, the agent is not able to do otherwise. Also, knowledge that is derived from an agent's nature would be a part of God's

---

[20] Flint, *Divine Providence*, 85, 123–125, 127. Flint acknowledges that much is not known regarding how grounding works but that Molinists will not wish to claim ignorance. See also Alvin Plantinga, "Replies," in *Alvin Plantinga*, ed. James Tomberlin and Peter van Inwagen (Dordrecht, Netherlands: D. Reidel, 1985), 378.

[21] Craig, *The Only Wise God*, 119–123; David Basinger, "Middle Knowledge and Classical Christian Thought," *RS* 22 (1986): 421. Craig argues that objections to Molinism imply a Truth-maker theory of truth for counterfactuals, but such a theory is not proven. Counterfactuals of freedom may be brute facts. See also William Lane Craig, "Middle Knowledge, Truth-Makers, and the 'Grounding Objection,'" *FP* 18 (2001): 337–352; idem, "Ducking Friendly Fire: Davison on the Grounding Objection," *PC* 8 (2006): 165–166.

The Molinist Solution

natural knowledge, not middle knowledge, since natural knowledge deals with necessities of nature. As a result, counterfactuals of freedom grounded in an agent's nature could only be free in a compatibilist sense. Because Molinism denies that compatibilist freedom is real freedom, Kvanvig's theory is unacceptable as a method of grounding and knowing true counterfactuals of freedom.

Freddoso and Flint both argue that the truth of counterfactuals of freedom can be grounded in the future occurrence of the circumstance stated by the counterfactual of freedom. Just as statements about the past are grounded because past events occurred, true statements about the future are grounded because future events will occur. Thus, counterfactuals of freedom can be known. This argument is based on the claim that the correspondence theory of truth does not need the existence of any ontological grounds in order for there to be truth to a counterfactual of freedom. Such a claim, however, seems strange since the correspondence theory of truth is defined by the possession of a correspondence relation to reality, and it seems that there is no reality to which true counterfactuals of freedom may correspond. The circumstance the counterfactual indicates does not yet exist. The agent does not yet exist. Therefore, how can it be true? No correspondence relation exits to make it true. Further, counterfactuals of freedom cannot be grounded in the divine nature or the divine will because that would remove libertarian freedom.

True counterfactuals of freedom can also fail to obtain. These non-obtaining counterfactuals would have a truth value but no future event to ground their truth. How then are they true? Without such a relation to a reality, it is difficult to see how truth can exist for counterfactuals of freedom logically and temporally prior to the existence of the circumstances stated by the counterfactual. Further, it is difficult to see how true counterfactuals of freedom that fail to obtain can have a truth value when that truth value is dependent on the obtaining of a future event. Thus, Freddoso and Flint's position does not appear viable.

Freddoso and Flint's position has several other issues that make it questionable. According to Steve Cowan, past-tensed statements have a truth grounded in events that have been actualized. The events for future statements have no truth ground in temporal reality as past statements do. The claim "z is now grounded" was true before the claim "it was the case that z"; however, the claim "it will be the case that z" is said to be true before the claim "z is now grounded." These situations are not parallel as Flint and Freddoso claim. Past-tensed statements are different from future tense statements because the ground for past tense statements already existed. The ground for future tense statements does not yet exist. As a result, the treatment of the grounding of these two types of statements cannot be parallel with each other.[22]

Timothy O'Connor asserts that Flint and Freddoso's claim concerning the grounding of counterfactuals is incorrect. First, the term "ground" is being used to imply that something exists in reality now to provide grounding and truth, which is false. Thus, one can only say that a future-tensed proposition or counterfactual of freedom is true just in case its present tense counterpart will have grounds at a future time. In fact, it turns out that no future tense proposition or counterfactual of freedom can presently have grounds. Therefore, these counterfactuals cannot have a truth value. Second, Freddoso's claim that a future tense proposition and counterfactuals of freedom will have grounds is itself future-tensed. This fact leads to an infinite regress, for Freddoso's claim about the future grounding of future-tensed propositions and counterfactuals of freedom receives its truth only if its present-tensed counterpart will be true. The claim that its counterpart will be true is itself future-tensed and can only be true if its present-tensed counterpart will be true. Since that counterpart is also future-tensed and needs a future ground, a regress of grounding is established.[23] As a result, it does not appear that Freddoso and Flint's appeal to circumstances that will occur can be a proper method for knowing counterfactuals of freedom.

Dekker's contention is that true counterfactuals of freedom are grounded in the agent's action. Although counterfactuals of freedom are true logically prior to the existence of the agent, the agent and his actions simultaneously exist along with the counterfactual. Thus, the agent brings about but does not cause the truth of the counterfactual rather than the true counterfactual bringing about the action. Dekker's position, however, appears to be circular and fallacious. Counterfactuals of freedom possess their truth value logically prior to the existence of the agent and his action. Even though the truth of counterfactuals of freedom may be temporally simultaneous with the agent's action, the truth of the existence of the agent and his action asymmetrically depends on the truth of the counterfactual of freedom, not the other way around. God creates circumstances according to the truth of the counterfactuals of freedom, and agents act as these counterfactuals indicate. In Dekker's argument, agents determine the truth value of counterfactuals of freedom

---

22 Steve Cowan, "The Grounding Objection to Middle Knowledge Revisited," *RS* 39 (2003): 96–97.
23 Timothy O'Connor, "The Impossibility of Middle Knowledge," *PS* 68 (1992): 155–156, 158.

through their actions. God then uses his knowledge of the counterfactuals of freedom to create the agent and his circumstance. The agent then acts as the counterfactuals of freedom indicate while also determining the truth of these counterfactuals so that God may create by them. This account is circular. As a result, Dekker's position makes no sense. How is God able to arrange the future according to his middle knowledge when what he knows is determined by what he creates? Thus, Dekker's argument results in circularity, which is unacceptable.

Dekker's claims also face another major hurdle. Dekker argues that the truth of counterfactuals of freedom can be grounded in counterfactual freedom. If the agent would have acted differently, then God would have believed differently. Pike argues, however, that this claim does not demonstrate that things can be different. God would have believed differently if an agent would have acted differently; however, this does not change the fact that the agent will not act differently such that God's knowledge will be different. The counterfactuals of freedom are still true, and the agent will still act as the counterfactuals indicate. If something else had happened, God would have believed otherwise, but the agent cannot do other than what is foreknown by the counterfactuals of freedom. These counterfactuals and the foreknowledge they produce are now necessary, so it does not matter what one would have done or what God would have believed.[24] It is not in an agent's power to do otherwise or change the truth of his counterfactuals of freedom. If Dekker's view is right, an agent cannot be free in the libertarian sense. Since such a power to change counterfactuals of freedom and act otherwise in any circumstance cannot be performed by an agent, appealing to counterfactual freedom as a ground is unsatisfactory.

As a result, the Molinist is left with the contention that counterfactuals of freedom are just brute, unexplained facts. They have no ground for their truth value and do not need to be grounded. They simply exist and possess their truth value. As a result, God knows counterfactuals of freedom innately within his creation situation. Since this position appears to be the only viable position for Molinism, any application of the Molinist Solution to the divine situation must incorporate this understanding of counterfactuals of freedom.

Divine Freedom and the Molinist Solution

How could a brute facts model of counterfactuals of freedom be applied to the divine situation? Like human beings, God is a free agent who can act in a

---

24 See Nelson Pike, *God and Timelessness* (Routledge and Kegan Paul, 1970), 58.

variety of ways and circumstances. As a result, it is possible that counterfactuals of freedom exist that assert what God would freely do in any circumstance. Given that such true counterfactuals of divine freedom exist, God can know exactly how he would freely act in any situation, including how he would act within the creation situation in which he finds himself. These counterfactuals of divine freedom must be brute facts that God innately knows. Their existence and truth are not based in the divine nature or in God's future actions. Further, God cannot bring about the existence and truth of these counterfactuals of divine freedom. They exist and are true logically prior to God's acting. Since this knowledge would be logically prior to his choice and action, God would have exhaustive foreknowledge of his own free choices and actions. For any circumstance that obtains, God knows exactly how he would freely respond in that circumstance. In arranging counterfactuals of human freedom, God also arranges the counterfactuals of divine freedom. Further, God's creation situation is a counterfactual situation since it could have been different. It too has a counterfactual claim; therefore, God innately knows how he would freely arrange the counterfactuals of freedom in that creation situation. As a result, God is able to completely know his own future via the counterfactuals of divine freedom without threatening divine freedom. It seems then that the problem of foreknowledge and divine freedom might be solved by appealing to counterfactuals of divine freedom.

There are major questions regarding the contention that there are brute fact counterfactuals of divine freedom and their potential use as a solution to the problem of foreknowledge and divine freedom. First, whether or not counterfactuals of divine and human freedom can be known by God at all is unclear. Though I have argued that the brute fact model is the best model for understanding how God knows counterfactuals of freedom, this model may not be viable either. Counterfactuals of freedom seem to need something to correspond to in order to be true, but to what do they correspond? They are not categorical prophecies that are true and must occur; otherwise, counterfactuals that are never actualized by God would be false prophecies. Since some counterfactuals of freedom are not made actual but remain true, they do not qualify as categorical prophecies. One cannot appeal to causal or logical laws because that would necessitate the agent's action and remove libertarian freedom. Since counterfactuals of freedom are supposed to uphold the libertarian freedom of an agent, such an appeal to logic or causation as the source of correspondence is unavailable. One also cannot appeal to intentions, desires, and character of an agent as the source of correspondence since agents often act against these things. Further, an agent's character, intentions, and desires cannot specify how an agent would act since it would remove libertarian freedom; therefore, an agent's character, intentions, and desires are not proper grounds for correspondence. It appears that there is no available reality to which counterfactuals of freedom may correspond. Without any reality to which counterfactuals of freedom may correspond, it does not appear that these counterfactuals of freedom can be true and known. God could know what an agent would probably do in a counterfactual situation, but he could not know what the agent would definitely do.[25] If God cannot have certain knowledge of the truth of these counterfactuals of freedom, then God can know neither his nor any created creature's future by knowing the counterfactuals of freedom. Middle knowledge is ineffective at knowing the future of an agent.

The brute facts model is supposed to relieve this tension between the grounding of the truth of counterfactuals of freedom and God's awareness of them. Counterfactuals of freedom simply exist and are true without the need for a correspondence relation to reality. Further, they are innately possessed by God. However, is the brute fact model even viable? It does not appear to be so. Molinists argue that the content of God's middle knowledge could have been different. According to Molinism, counterfactuals of freedom are not caused to be true by anything internal or external to God. On the brute fact model, it seems that nothing causes God to know counterfactuals of freedom versus not knowing them.[26] On the other hand, if the content of God's middle knowledge can be different, then these counterfactuals of freedom do not possess their truth value necessarily. As a result, these counterfactual truths must be accidentally possessed by God because they are not essentially possessed by him. They do not reside as part of God's natural knowledge and cannot be essentially possessed by God. God then must obtain his knowledge of counterfactuals of freedom because he does not possess knowledge of them essentially by nature. As a result, it seems that counterfactuals of freedom must have a cause for their truth value since they do not have to possess their truth value. Since they begin be true, they must have a cause for their truth.

Appealing to mysterious brute facts, however, does not explain how one set of counterfactuals of freedom is true over another set. They just happen to be true and known by God. If this is the case, then the content of God's middle knowledge just happens to be what it is. How can God innately possess

---

25 Robert Adams, *The Virtue of Faith* (Oxford University Press, 1987), 80–81, 113–114; William Hasker, *God, Time, and Knowledge* (Cornell University Press, 1989), 20, 24–25, 27–29, 31, 36–38; Kenny, *The God of the Philosophers*, 68–71; Steven Cowan, "The Grounding Objection to Middle Knowledge Revisited," *RS* 39 (2003): 94.

26 Joshua Hoffman and Gary Rosenkrantz, *The Divine Attributes* (Blackwell, 2002), 81–82.

knowledge of counterfactuals of freedom of any kind when it is unclear how they even come to be true and known by God? As Joshua Hoffman and Gary Rosenkrantz argue, there seems to be no cognitive process for obtaining the truths of middle knowledge. Truths of middle knowledge are not obtained by introspection, perception, the *a priori*, intuition, deduction, induction, or memory. In the end, such knowledge is mysteriously, if not magically, possessed by God.[27] It seems as though the Molinist view cannot provide an adequate model for middle knowledge of counterfactuals of freedom, including counterfactuals of divine freedom. The brute facts model does not appear to be a valid method for grounding the existence of the truth of counterfactuals of freedom.

The brute facts model faces other problems as well. Other critics note that such appeals to brute facts are immune to important questions of logic: namely how they are true.[28] To some, the brute fact argument seems desperate, even though it is a possible move. Other propositions can be grounded, so it is more plausible that counterfactuals of freedom need a ground than not.[29] As a result, an appeal to brute fact knowledge takes on the appearance of being *ad hoc*. Counterfactuals of freedom are supposed to be contingent in their truth, but as brute facts, there seems to be no explanation as to how they could have been different. Neither human beings nor God can make them different. In fact, there is nothing that can determine whether they are true or not. If nothing determines the truth of counterfactuals of human and divine freedom, it is difficult to see how they are contingent in their truth. If these counterfactuals of freedom cannot be different in their truth, then the Molinist position is undermined as well as divine and human libertarian freedom.[30] As a result, the brute fact explanation of counterfactuals of freedom does not appear to ground the truth of any counterfactuals of freedom or to support the Molinist framework.

A final and potentially devastating criticism of the brute fact model is that the brute fact model appears to relieve anyone of being responsible for the truth of counterfactuals of freedom or for the actions that they do which correspond to those counterfactuals. In fact, the brute fact model appears to demonstrate that an agent only has the power to bring about true counterfactuals of freedom. He cannot bring about any false counterfactuals of freedom or any non-existing counterfactuals of freedom, since only the brute counter-

---

27 Ibid., 123.
28 David Gordon and Michael Sadowsky, "Does Theism Need Middle Knowledge," *RS* 25 (1989): 87.
29 Cowan, "Grounding Objection," 98–99.
30 Rogers, *Perfect Being*, 82–83.

factuals of freedom exist and have truth. Thus, the agent is not really free in the libertarian sense because he cannot do otherwise.[31] Since counterfactuals of divine freedom would also be brute facts, then God could only bring about true counterfactuals of divine freedom. He would not have the power to bring about false counterfactuals of divine freedom. It seems that brute counterfactuals of divine freedom would actually determine God's actions rather than make them free.

If there are counterfactuals of freedom as Molinism claims, then it seems impossible that God should even know them since there is no manner for him to know them. If God cannot know counterfactuals of freedom, including counterfactuals of divine freedom, then he certainly cannot exhaustively know the future of any agent including himself. It seems that a Molinist account ends up denying the possible foreknowledge of both human and divine action. The Molinist position might be buttressed if counterfactuals of freedom were equated with the divine ideas, but the divine ideas are a part of God's natural knowledge, not his middle knowledge. The divine ideas are an essential aspect of the divine nature. Thus, they are essential to God's knowledge, not contingent. In addition, the divine ideas may not support the libertarian conception of freedom that counterfactuals of freedom require. The divine ideas require that God act in specific ways within possible worlds. As a result, the divine ideas may not allow God to do otherwise.

Another criticism of the Molinist position is that it appears to imply that counterfactuals of divine freedom would need to be arranged so that God could know not only his own future but also the futures of creatures. In order to know the future free actions of creatures, God needs to arrange counterfactuals of creaturely freedom. God, however, cannot arrange such creaturely counterfactuals until his own counterfactuals of freedom have been arranged because counterfactuals of divine freedom guide how God will arrange counterfactuals of creaturely freedom. This implication can be interpreted in two ways. First, the arrangement of the divine counterfactuals of freedom implies that God makes choices regarding the arrangement of the counterfactuals of divine freedom. However, these logically prior choices regarding the arrangement of divine counterfactuals are also divine counterfactual situations. Since it is a divine counterfactual situation, then the counterfactuals for these choices will need arranging as well, which implies another logically prior choice by God. This further logically prior choice is a divine counterfactual situation that needs arrangement by God, and so on. Such a model cre-

---

31 Hasker, *God, Time, and Knowledge*, 49–51.

ates an infinite regress of counterfactual situations for God to arrange, which is absurd.

Second, the counterfactuals of divine freedom could be arranged by some other being or reality. This interpretation appears to be exactly what Molinism would embrace. As the Molinist position claims, there is a creation situation in which God happens to reside. This situation contains a specific set of counterfactuals of freedom. According to Molinism, the set of counterfactuals of freedom can be different. As a result, God's creation situation can be different. It then appears that the counterfactuals of divine freedom exist and can be arranged by the reality of the creation situation in which God finds himself. Given these assertions, the question that must be asked is how God finds himself in a specific creation situation. What determines that God be in this creation situation rather than in another? Further, how does God come to know the creation situation in which he resides along with its corresponding counterfactuals of freedom?

Clearly, God cannot determine the creation situation in which he resides. If he did, then a creation situation would exist logically prior to the creation situation that he determines. The existence of that preexisting creation situation would need explaining, supposedly by God's creation of that preexisting creation situation. However, this would lead to another logically prior creation situation that needs explaining, and the infinite regress of creating creation situations begins.[32] On the other hand, if God does not determine the creation situation in which he resides, then certain unsavory consequences follow. First, there must be some source external to God that determines the creation situation in which he resides. If this is so, then God is neither *a se* nor completely sovereign. He is dependent on some other higher power for the manner of his existence, but this conclusion is surely false. God cannot depend on something higher than himself because there is nothing higher than God.

Second, the possibility that God could exist in different creation situations implies that such situations are not a natural and essential feature of the divine existence. They would be accidental. This accidental existence further implies that God comes to be in a specific creation situation in which he did not previously exist; otherwise, he would eternally exist in his essential creation situation, denying the possibility that he could exist in a different one. Since there is nothing higher than God that could determine which cre-

---

32 David Gordon and James Sadowsky make a similar argument as the one presented here regarding divine counterfactuals of freedom. If such counterfactuals exist, then God must determine them which would require counterfactuals of freedom for that determining choice, etc. See Gordon and Sadowsky, "Does Theism Need Middle Knowledge," 82–85.

ation situation he resides in, it seems that God must always have existed in his creation situation and have been determined by it. There would then be only one logically possible creation situation in which God can exist. If this were so, then there is only one logically possible set of divine and creaturely counterfactuals of freedom, which is counter to what Molinism claims.

Third, God would not have been able to act in any other way since there is neither an alternative creation situation in which he could have existed nor other counterfactuals of freedom to confront him. The creation situation specifies that God would create in this manner and no other. Thus, there is only one logically possible way in which God would creatively act and respond to his creation as determined by his creation situation. As a result, middle knowledge of counterfactuals of human and divine freedom degrades into natural knowledge. This destroys the Molinist framework for freedom both for God and man while implying logical fatalism. Since there is no means by which God can be in a different creation situation, then it is not logically possible that he exists in a different creation situation. Thus, it is logically necessary that God create according to the arrangement of the counterfactuals of divine and human freedom that his creation situation specifies.

The interpretation that God's counterfactuals of divine freedom are arranged for him is inimical not only to the definition of God since he is the greatest being and highest reality but also to his freedom. Nothing is beyond God that could arrange his counterfactuals of freedom. As a result, it seems that God is stuck in a certain divine counterfactual situation. He cannot decide whether he resides within that situation or not. Thus, a Molinist model of counterfactuals of divine freedom does not allow for God to choose to reside within different counterfactual situations. Further, he is not free to act in a manner different from the dictates of his creation situation. Knowledge of such a counterfactual situation will also be essential to the divine being since there is nothing that can make that counterfactual situation different; therefore, God cannot act differently than what he knows his counterfactual creation situation specifies, and fatalism follows.

A final criticism is that counterfactuals of freedom deny the very freedom that Molinism is attempting to uphold. As Steve Cowan argues using what he calls the Generic Grounding Objection, Molinism is impossible given the libertarian freedom it wishes to defend. Assuming that an agent is free in any circumstance (not determined) to do x or ~x, Cowan claims that there can be no fact regarding what the agent would do in any circumstance. If an agent is free in this sense, there can be no truth or falsity as to what an agent would do. It is simply indeterminate. Nothing about the agent, the circumstance, or the action could provide grounds for the truth of the counterfactual of freedom.[33]

If the claims of Molinism are incompatible with libertarian freedom, then it seems that Molinism actually repudiates the sense of freedom it is attempting to defend. Hoffman and Rosenkrantz make a similar argument. The Molinist's counterfactuals of freedom are supposed to demonstrate subjunctive conditionals that do not imply physical or logical causation; however, given that they stress what would happen, counterfactuals of freedom assert a connection between the parts of the counterfactual: the antecedent and the consequent. If the agent is placed in those circumstances, then he has no choice but to perform a specific action. This conclusion denies libertarian freedom; therefore, Hoffman and Rosenkrantz claim that Molinism is inconsistent.[34]

In a similar way, Robert Adams argues that counterfactuals of freedom, God's decision to create, and human existence are all explanatorily prior to human free action. He then argues that explanatory priority is both transitive and asymmetrical. No human choice is explanatorily prior to the counterfactuals of freedom; therefore, the agent's actions are not the grounds of these counterfactuals of freedom.[35] Using explanatory priority, Adams argues that all counterfactuals of freedom have a truth value prior to an agent's actual choice. The agent does not cause or make the counterfactual of freedom true; however, a libertarianly free agent's action must be explanatorily prior to any truth about it. The agent is not libertarianly free regarding the actions specified by the counterfactual of freedom. Since there can be no truth inconsistent with the agent's action explanatorily prior to the act, then one must act according to what that truth dictates. The agent cannot do otherwise, which violates libertarian freedom. Libertarianly free actions cannot be sufficiently explained, which is why no truth inconsistent with a libertarianly free act can be explanatorily prior to the action.[36]

If no counterfactual of freedom can imply libertarian freedom, then counterfactuals of divine freedom cannot imply libertarian freedom. Counterfactuals of divine freedom exist logically prior to God and are not made true by him. Since God's libertarianly free action is not the ground for divine counter-

---

33 Cowan, "Grounding Objection," 94.

34 Hoffman and Rosenkrantz, *The Divine Attributes*, 121–122. See Cowan, "Grounding Objection," 100; O'Connor, "The Impossibility of Middle Knowledge," 159–162. See also William Hasker, "A Refutation of Middle Knowledge," *Nous* 20 (1986): 553–556; idem, "A New Anti-Molinist Argument," *RS* 35 (1999): 291–297.

35 Robert Adams, "An Anti-Molinist Argument," *PP* 5 (1991): 346–347.

36 Ibid., 249–250, 352. See also William Hasker, "Anti-Molinism is Undefeated!" *FP* 17 (2000): 128–129; idem, "Explanatory Priority: Transitive and Unequivocal, A Reply to William Craig," *PPR* 56 (1997): 389–393.

factuals of freedom, then God cannot be libertarianly free in any action since he cannot do other than what his counterfactuals of freedom indicate. As a result, counterfactuals of divine and human freedom can only imply compatibilist freedom. Since Molinists claim that libertarian freedom is the only real kind of freedom, God's actions cannot be free if there are true counterfactuals about his acting. This criticism stands even if satisfactory explanations were found for the criticisms of the brute fact model and creation situations. Just because counterfactuals of freedom can be different and can be innately known does not imply that the counterfactuals in themselves are compatible with the agent's libertarian freedom. Thus, Molinism cannot defend a version of divine freedom that implies indeterminism.

Conclusion

In the end, Molinism cannot be an adequate solution to the problem of foreknowledge and divine freedom. First, Molinism appears to be compatible only with the brute facts model of counterfactuals of freedom. This model, however, is highly suspect as a means for grounding and knowing counterfactuals of freedom. Further, such brute counterfactuals may not be able to allow for libertarian freedom. Second, Molinism robs God of his sovereign control and freedom by placing him at the mercy of the creation situation in which he resides. Since counterfactuals of divine freedom cannot be different because God's creation situation cannot be different, then God can act in only one specific way, implying logical fatalism. Third, counterfactuals of freedom, even divine ones, do not seem to imply the truth of libertarian freedom. Agents cannot act in ways other than how counterfactuals of freedom indicate. Thus, Molinism is inconsistent with its own claims.

As a result, the Molinist Solution does not comply with the criteria established for a successful solution to the problem of foreknowledge and divine freedom. Brute counterfactuals of freedom do not appear to be things that God can know; therefore, Molinism does not demonstrate that God can know the future. The Molinist Solution also implies logical fatalism since God's creation situation and its counterfactual claims both upon him and human beings cannot be different. Further, the inability of counterfactuals of freedom to imply libertarian freedom suggests that agents, like God, are either logically or naturally necessitated by these counterfactuals. As a result, the Molinist Solution violates the first and second criteria for a satisfactory solution to the problem of foreknowledge and divine freedom. Under the weight of these criticisms, I conclude that Molinism fails as a potential solution.

CHAPTER 5

THE OCKHAMIST SOLUTION

Since the Open Solution and the Molinist Solution have been rejected as inadequate for adjudicating the problem of foreknowledge and divine freedom, I now turn to a more unique approach to the issue. This chapter examines the Ockhamist Solution to the problem of foreknowledge and freedom to see if it can be successfully applied to the problem of divine freedom. Though there is only one basic theory to this solution, there are several views that emphasize different aspects of the solution. The first section examines the basic theory which belongs to Ockham himself. The second section examines modern appropriations of the Ockhamist position particularly the Hard-Soft Fact Distinction as well as the issue of an agent's power over the past. I argue that none of these views are successful in providing an adequate solution to problem of foreknowledge and divine freedom.

OCKHAM'S SOLUTION

William of Ockham claims that his solution to the problem of foreknowledge and human freedom defends the power to act indifferently, or libertarian freedom. One is both able to cause and not to cause the same effect when there is no difference in anything outside that power (i.e. no change in circumstance). Ockham claims that no matter how much reason dictates something, the will is still able to will, to refrain from willing, or to will against.[1] Ockham thus holds to a standard definition of libertarian freedom as the only

---

[1] William of Ockham, *Quodlibeta Questions*, vol. 1, trans. Alfred Freddoso and Francis Kelly (Yale University Press, 1991), 1.16.

kind of freedom. How then does Ockham propose to show that freedom is compatible with God's omniscience, which includes knowledge of the future?

Ockham begins by stating that he holds to bivalence. Ockham rejects Aristotle's position against the principle of bivalence and excluded middle and insists that God knows all things with certainty, although he claims that he does not know how God possesses this certain knowledge. Ockham also rejects Duns Scotus' position that bivalence and excluded middle are established logically posterior to the divine will. Scotus' position is that logically prior to the divine will, certain propositions were neutral in their truth value. First, Ockham sees Scotus' claim as a denial of libertarian freedom for the creature since any proposition about how the creature will act is now determinately true and cannot be different. The creature must act in a certain way as settled by the divine will. Secondly, Ockham argues that when something is determined contingently where it is possible that it is not determined and could never have been determined (as with the divine will), then one cannot have certain knowledge of it. Such certain knowledge is impossible for God. Thus, Ockham asserts that it is impossible to know how God knows things contingently and with certainty, but he must know since the saints and the faith require such a belief.[2]

Ockham also holds to the position that propositions cannot now change their truth value; however, he also rejects the position that one proposition being true means its opposite cannot obtain and must be false. Rather, both propositions are contingent, could obtain, and could have a different truth value. A contingent proposition that is true now could have been false and vice versa; thus, what is false could have obtained. If it had been false, then it would have been true to say that it never was true to begin with. Once a proposition's truth value is settled, it does not change; however, its truth value could have been different.[3] From these claims, Ockham concludes that certain past, present, and future-tensed propositions about the future are contingent since they could be either false or true.[4]

Ockham also holds that propositions can be made determinately true or false as time passes, particularly regarding the time to which the proposition refers. Any present tense proposition is determinately false until the present time that the proposition asserts when it is made determinately true. Subsequently, the proposition is false again after the present moment has passed. For example, *Moses lives now* was determinately false before Moses' birth,

---
2 Ibid., 1.A6.
3 William of Ockham, *Predestination, God's Foreknowledge, and Future Contingents*, trans. Marilyn Adams and Norman Kretzmann (Meredith Corporation, 1969), 1.5–6.
4 Ockham, *Predestination*, 1.A2.

true while he lived, and false after he died. Any future tense proposition is indeterminate in its truth value until the future time stated by the proposition. Once that time obtains, the proposition is determinate in its truth value but only as it relates to a specific time. *Moses will part the Red Sea at t* was indeterminately true until Moses parted the Red Sea at *t*. According to Ockham, these changes are merely changes in the creation and not changes in God's knowledge. A proposition may be true at one time and false at another, but God knows their truth value at any time.[5]

How do these claims relate to the problem of foreknowledge and free will? To answer this question, Ockham claims that propositions about the present have a corresponding past-tensed proposition that is fixed in its truth. The proposition *I am typing now* has a corresponding past tense proposition, *I typed at t*, which is fixed in its truth. There are some propositions, however, that are about the future and do not have a corresponding past-tensed proposition that is fixed in its truth. *I will go to Paris at t* does not have a corresponding past-tensed proposition (*I went to Paris at t*) that is fixed in its truth since I have yet to actualize going to Paris at *t*. There are even true propositions about the past and the future that do not have an accompanying true proposition in the present tense. *I went to Paris at t* has no true present tense counterpart (*I am going to Paris now*) because I am not going to Paris now. *I will go to Paris at t* has no true present tense counterpart because I have yet to actualize going to Paris at *t*. Ockham claims that any proposition past or present in tense whose subject matter involves the future is contingent because the proposition depends upon the truth of future events for its truth. It only has a corresponding proposition about the past that is contingently true.[6]

As William Lane Craig puts it, Ockham believes that future contingent propositions are dependent on time. They are determinately true or false because the states of affairs to which they correspond will determinately be actually present or not be actually present. Future contingent propositions are thus based in present tense propositions that are presently true. They are true or false as they correspond to states of affairs that obtain in the world. Once the appropriate time stated by the proposition obtains, the proposition is no longer contingent in its truth. This is not to say that such propositions can change truth value but rather that they could have possessed a different truth

---

5 Ibid., 2.3.1. See also Gordon Leff, *William of Ockham* (Manchester University Press, 1975), 450–452; and Philotheus Boehner, *Collected Articles on Ockham*, ed. Eligius Buytaert (Franciscan Institute, 1958), 37–40.

6 Ockham, *Predestination*, 1.A3–4. See also Calvin Normore, "Divine Omniscience, Omnipotence, and Future Contingents: An Overview," in *Divine Omniscience and Omnipotence in Medieval Philosophy*, ed. Tamar Rudavsky (D. Reidel, 1985), 13–14.

value. They could have always been different than what in fact they are. This possibility of being true or false until the state of affairs obtains is what Ockham calls necessity *per accidens*. Prior to the obtaining of the state of affairs in the proposition, that state of affairs could have obtained or failed to obtain. Once the state of affairs obtained, then the state of affairs could not fail to obtain. The state of affairs accidentally gained necessary existence by obtaining. This type of necessity is not logical necessity or causal necessity. It refers only to the necessity that is gained in time once a state of affairs obtains at a temporal moment.[7] Up until a future time t, a future-tensed proposition is contingently true. Once the state of affairs it references obtains, the proposition cannot fail to be true. Its truth is accidentally necessary.

For Ockham, propositions about the contingent future are true and known by God, but they are only contingently determined in their truth and known by God. Future contingent propositions, therefore, have a truth value but are not necessary *per accidens*. God's foreknowledge depends on these future states of affairs being actualized in order for them to be known. Since things could be otherwise, any foreknown future contingent proposition is temporally contingent until the future state of affairs obtains. God knows with certainty which future contingent propositions are true, but it is not necessary *per accidens* that he know them. Up until the time that the state of affairs obtains, God could have known differently. A future contingent proposition that is true cannot be made false, but up until the time that the future state of affairs obtains, the proposition could have been false. For example, *I will be five feet, nine inches tall at t* was a true proposition prior to my obtaining that height at t. If I would have lost my legs in an accident before obtaining that height at t, then the proposition would have been false. The proposition could have been false until the event obtains, but it cannot fail to be true once the event obtains. Thus, the content of God's knowledge must be contingent as the proposition is contingent in its truth. God cannot change, but his entire history could have been different. Since the content of God's knowledge is asymmetrically certified by the future events, God's knowledge could have been different so long as future events are still un-actualized. Once the events are actualized, then it is impossible that God's knowledge be other than it is.[8]

Thus, Ockham affirms the claims that future contingents can be settled in their truth value so that God can know them. Human deliberation is not in vain since it is logically possible that agents do otherwise. Even if God knows

---

[7] William Lane Craig, *The Problem of Divine Foreknowledge*, 148–150.

[8] Ibid, 151–152, 154, 155, 167. See also Marilyn Adams, *William Ockham*, vol. 2 (University of Notre Dame, 1987), 1141–1145, and Zagzebski, *Dilemma of Freedom and Foreknowledge*, 68.

the future, God could bring about an opposite future if his history had been different. Ockham rests these affirmations on his distinction that while God knows all future contingent propositions as true, he knows them as contingently determined. These propositions could have been different in their truth value; therefore, future contingent propositions have truth value and have it contingently. God could have failed to know any future contingent proposition as true. He could have known it as false. Human deliberation matters because it affects what will obtain and become necessary *per accidens*, and God is not limited in his knowledge and power to only one possible way of acting.[9] Ockham concludes that this distinction in the nature of propositions, their necessity *per accidens*, and their relative truth values allow people to express libertarian freedom and have some say in what God ultimately knows.

Modern Interpretations

Modern Ockhamists recognize that the past cannot be changed; however, they claim that some propositions are not wholly about the past. As a result, they concentrate on determining which events are really in the past. All modern Ockhamist interpretations seek to be consistent with this distinction between facts. There cannot be counterexamples that ruin the distinction and demonstrate that God's past beliefs are in the past and accidentally necessary.[10] There are two broad types of modern Ockhamist interpretations. The first distinguishes between hard and soft facts and shows that God's past beliefs about the future fall into the soft category. The second defines accidental necessity in terms of what is in an agent's power to do. This interpretation must pick out a class of facts that is not logically or causally necessary yet an agent cannot alter them. Facts that are accidentally necessary are neither logically or causally necessary. They are facts about which nothing can be done at a certain time. God's past beliefs about the future are not said to be such facts.[11]

The Hard-Soft Fact Distinction

One way modern Ockhamists explain how future-tensed propositions have truth but have it contingently is the Hard-Soft Fact Distinction. This distinc-

---

9 Ockham, *Predestination*, 2.1.
10 Zagzebski, *Dilemma of Freedom and Foreknowledge*, 71, 74. Zagzebski calls this view the Fixed Past Constraint Principle.
11 Ibid., 67. Zagzebski believes that no one has been successful in these endeavors.

tion was first applied by Marilyn Adams. She defines a soft fact and a hard fact as the following:

(SF): any statement *p* is at least in part about a time *t* where the happening or not happening, actuality or non-actuality of something at *t* is a necessary condition of the truth of *p*.

(HF): a statement *p* about a time *t* where *p* is not at least in part about any time future relative to *t*.[12]

For example, the statement *God knows that Jones will mow his lawn at noon tomorrow* is a soft fact according to Adams since the truth of the entire statement is dependent on the condition that Jones actually mows his law at noon tomorrow. Since this statement is partly about the future relative to God's knowledge, whether it is true depends on the future events actually obtaining. On the other hand, the statement *God knows that Jones mowed his lawn yesterday at noon* is a hard fact. Since Jones' mowing is already actual and in the past relative to God's knowing, the entire statement is true and depends upon nothing to obtain in the future in order to be true. Because soft facts depend on the obtaining of future events, an agent may have the power to bring them about. If this claim is true, the Hard-Soft Fact Distinction may solve the problem of foreknowledge and freedom. Since the hard fact has obtained, the freedom of the act is no longer an issue. The action is done and cannot be changed, so the agent lacks freedom concerning that action. On the other hand, the truth of the soft fact depends on what the agent will do; therefore, the agent is not forced to act in a certain manner by the claims of the future-tensed contingent proposition. Thus, the agent is considered to be free since his action is not forced upon him and he could do otherwise. If the agent were to act otherwise, then God would have known differently from all eternity past. The agent, however, will not do otherwise since the soft fact is still determinately, though contingently, true.

To demonstrate the veracity of these definitions, Adams appeals to the concept of everlasting existence. She argues that any definition concerning this concept implies that God exists at all times, even future ones; therefore, everlasting existence is a soft fact about God's existence since it contains claims concerning times other than the present on which the truth of ever-

---

12 Marilyn Adams, "Is the Existence of God a 'Hard' Fact?" *PR* 76 (1967): 493–494. Adams here develops the hard-soft distinction that Pike references in "Of God and Freedom: A Rejoinder," *PR* 75 (1966): 369–379.

lasting existence rests. The claim that God exists at some time does not state a hard fact about the time in which he exists. As a result, Adams claims that a person does not possess the power to make it such that God failed to exist at an earlier time. Since any agent can make claims concerning times connected to God's everlasting existence not obtain, then they can make it such that God did not exist at that time. Adams applies the same argument to God's omniscience. Since God has beliefs about the future, then those beliefs are soft facts. As a result, a person has the power to bring it about that God held a different belief than he did. Again, God's everlasting existence is not a hard fact. One has the power to act so that the past is other than it was.[13]

Another set of definitions comes from Joshua Hoffman and Gary Rosenkrantz. They claim that propositions (or states of affairs) may be eternal in that they always obtain or fail to obtain (Socrates walked at t), or they may be unrestrictedly repeatable in that they may obtain, fail to obtain, then obtain again indefinitely (Socrates walks). Using this distinction, they define a hard fact as follows:

S is an unrestrictedly repeatable present (URP) state of affairs=def. (i) S is UR, and (ii) S is the present tense of a tenseless proposition.

A state of affairs r is a hard fact at a time t=def. (1) r is the state of affair S at (in) t; (2) S is a URP state of affairs; (3) S obtains throughout (throughout some part of) t; (4) either S is a simple state of affairs or if complex all its parts are URP; (5) neither r nor S nor any of S's parts entail a simple URP state of affairs indexed to a time which does not overlap with t or a complex URP state of affairs whose parts are URP and which is indexed to a time which does not overlap with t; and (6) t is a past time.[14]

---

13 Adams, "Is the Existence of God a 'Hard' Fact?," 495–498. Adams believes that Pike's argument errs in that Pike assumes that the ordinary concept of a person involves the essential identity of a person, God, to the properties that he possesses such that these properties and their exemplification make a person's existence a hard fact. If the person failed to exemplify these properties at any point in time, then he would not be the person that he is. Thus, an agent would fail to have any power over God's past existence since God's everlasting existence and all its implications are essential to his being. Adam's believes that her analysis of everlasting existence and omniscience shows that this conception of a person is flawed and unacceptable. Omniscience and everlasting existence are not essential to God since agents can affect their truth. See ibid., 500–501.

14 Joshua Hoffman and Gary Rosenkrantz, "Hard and Soft Facts," PR 93 (1984): 423, 425–426, 433. Hard facts are present-tensed because a past-tensed fact can be indexed to other times.

A hard fact is a present tense statement that is unrestrictedly repeatable, such as *Socrates walks*. It may obtain, fail to obtain, and then obtain again indefinitely. It is either simple, stating only one URP action, or is made up of simple URP actions. For example, *Socrates walks* is a singular simple, and *Socrates walks and eats* is a complex of simple parts. Hard facts also do not entail any time different from the time indicated by the statement. *Socrates walks* indicates no other time than the time of Socrates walking, whenever that may be. On the other hand, *Socrates walks at t* implies that Socrates walks at a specific time and did not begin walking at some later time relative to t. Lastly, a hard fact obtains at a past time, such as *Socrates walks* obtains at 430 BC. Since the actions in these kinds of statements have obtained and imply no other action at a future time, they are considered to be hard facts. Any statement whose specified action has not obtained or implies that the action or another action will obtain at a later time is a soft fact.

When applied to the problem of foreknowledge and freedom, Hoffman and Rosenkrantz claim that God's knowledge at t_1 of a person acting at t_2, where t_1 is earlier than t_2, fails to comply with the proposed definition of a hard fact. Since God necessarily exists and has essential omniscience, God's knowledge at t_1 cannot be URP since much of what he knows will be attached to a future time. This is a failure of (2), (4), and (6). Also, God's foreknowledge entails other facts about the agent in question, such as that he exists and that he acts. These entailments are URP and indexed to a time later than t_1, so they fail (5). Thus, Hoffman and Rosenkrantz claim that God's foreknowledge consists of contingent soft facts rather than necessary hard facts.[15] What God foreknows involves agents who exist and act at future times. This foreknowledge cannot be URP, cannot be simple, and implies events at other times. Since the agent's existence and action at those times logically could have been different, these foreknown facts are soft.

Another rendering of the hard-soft fact distinction comes from Alfred Freddoso. First, Freddoso claims that accidental necessity applies only to logically contingent propositions. Such propositions are necessary relative to a time t, remain necessary at all times after t, and are closed under entailment. Second, he emphasizes the primacy of the present for this distinction. What is true at any given moment t is true at t because of what has been, is, or will be purely present at t. As a result, a contingent claim is true at every moment at or after t in every possible world that shares the same history prior to t. This common history between possible worlds consists of shared present moments and their events. Each world has the same set of present moments up

---

15 Ibid., 429.

until the current present moment. Freddoso calls contingent claims about these present moments either immediate or non-immediate propositions.[16]

Because an immediate proposition is true in all possible worlds that share the same present moments as the actual world, they are accidentally necessary. A non-immediate proposition is one that is dependent on some other event at some other time later than the present moment. Since all possible worlds that share the same history up to t will not necessarily share all the same present moments after t, then all non-immediate propositions are not accidentally necessary.[17] For example, *God foreknows that Peter will deny Christ before the cock crows at t* is an immediate proposition since it is logically contingent that Peter denies Christ before the cock crows at t and this proposition is true in every possible world that shares the same history as the actual world up to the present moment of the actual world. Peter's action has obtained; therefore, the contingent proposition concerning his action is accidentally necessary and a hard fact in all worlds with a similar past history. On the other hand, *God foreknows that Jones will mow his lawn tomorrow* is a non-immediate proposition. This proposition is dependent on an event later than the present moment of the actual world, and it is not shared with all possible worlds identical to the history of the actual world up to the present moment. Jones fails to mow his lawn in some worlds that have the same past history up to the present moment. Since non-immediate propositions are not accidentally necessary, then they are not hard facts. Therefore, any non-immediate contingent proposition that God knows, he knows as a soft fact that is still contingent.

Lastly, Eddy Zemach and David Widerker have a slightly different understanding of the soft and hard fact distinction. They claim that a proposition is contingent if it possesses a truth value in the actual world and does or could possesses a different truth value in a world that is ontologically exact with this world. That is, this world belongs to the set of all possible worlds that share the same ontology with the actual world. A contingent proposition is accidentally necessary if it possesses the same truth value in every world that shares the same ontology with the actual world. Given this distinction, they claim that a soft fact is a proposition that is about the past and relative to a time t such that it is contingent. A hard fact is a proposition that is about the

---

16 Alfred Freddoso, "Accidental Necessity and Logical Determinism," in *God, Foreknowledge, and Freedom*, ed. John Martin Fischer (Stanford University Press, 1989), 138–139, 144, 146, 155–156. Freddoso has abandoned the Ockhamist position and currently supports the Molinist position.

17 Ibid., 154–156.

past and relative to a time t such that it is accidentally necessary.[18] Again, any contingent proposition about the future that God believes will be a soft fact and not accidentally necessary since the proposition could possess a different truth value in those worlds that are ontologically exact with the actual world.

Power Over the Past

Another major aspect of the Ockhamist view is to base the contingency of such propositions about the future in the power of an agent. John Turk Saunders argues that it is contradictory to hold that an agent has the ability to make God not exist. An agent also cannot make it such that God held a different belief or that God held a false belief. However, Saunders argues that the lack of these abilities does not provide reason to believe that an agent lacks the power to refrain from acting. While an agent can never perform an act that conflicts with God's beliefs, Saunders claims that this restriction does not entail that an agent lacks the ability to refrain. As Saunders explains, an agent can decide at t_1 to x at t_2, and the empirical law dictates that the agent will not change his mind. The agent still knows how to not-x and could perform not-x even though he will not change his mind. If the agent had done not-x, then the earlier situation would have been different and the empirical laws would have dictated differently. However, the agent's decision does not render him powerless to do not-x. The agent possesses this power even if he does not exercise it. The agent *could* exercise the power but *would* not do so. Again, this does not remove power. Power is only removed if the agent could not so act.[19] Saunders thinks that an agent's power to affect God's beliefs about the future is available to the agent even if he never exercises it.

Alvin Plantinga builds on this claim by applying it to the notion of accidental necessity. Plantinga admits that accidental necessity is a hard notion to understand but argues that it can be explained in terms of an agent's power to do or not do something. Plantinga contends that something that is accidentally necessary is something which is not within the power of any agent, even God, to change or affect.[20] Plantinga, however, argues that an agent can

---

18 Eddy Zemach and David Widerker, "Facts, Freedom, and Foreknowledge," in *God, Foreknowledge, and Freedom*, ed. John Martin Fischer (Stanford University Press, 1989), 114–115.
19 John Turk Saunders, "Of God and Freedom," *PR* 75 (1966): 219–222.
20 Alvin Plantinga, "On Ockham's Way Out," in *The Analytic Theist*, ed. James Sennett (Eerdmans 1998), 277–278, 283–287. See also Alfred Freddoso, "Accidental Necessity and Power Over the Past," *PPQ* 63 (1982): 54–68.

act such that if he had so acted, God would have held a different belief.[21] For Plantinga, future actions and events are within the power of agents to affect, so propositions about such future actions and events cannot be accidentally necessary. They must be contingent and known by God as contingent. Thus, agents have a power over the past to affect what God believed about the future at a past time. William Lane Craig argues that this is precisely what Ockham had in mind, though Ockham would not have held that an agent can actually change God's belief.[22] Whether the agent can actually change God's belief is ultimately beside the point. The point is that the future is contingent and in some sense dependent on the will of agents. This conclusion is all that is needed.

As has been discussed, the Ockhamist Solution looks to solve the problem of foreknowledge and human freedom by demonstrating how contingent propositions about the future can be true yet their truth value is contingent and dependent on agents and their future choices. Contingent propositions about future human actions do have a truth value and are known by God; however, these propositions about the future only possess their truth value contingently. They logically could have been different in their truth value. As a result, these future contingent propositions are considered to be soft facts that are dependent on the future actions of agents for their truth value. Ockhamists argue that human agents can act otherwise since these propositions about the future could have been different in their truth value. Agents could have acted otherwise such that God would have foreknown differently. How God would have foreknown differently is unknown, but agents do have libertarian freedom that can affect what God foreknows to some degree. Thus, the truth of future contingent propositions and God's knowledge of them depends on the human agent to some degree. The agent will not act in a way other than what these future contingent propositions state, but this should not be considered a loss of freedom for the agent. Instead, it is only a restraint in one's ability to act otherwise in some circumstance(s).

How could this argument be applied to the divine situation? One could argue that some propositions about God's future actions are true yet contin-

---

21 Alvin Plantinga, *God, Freedom, and Evil* (Eerdmans, 1974), 70–71.
22 William Lane Craig, "Temporal Necessity: Hard Facts/Soft Facts," *IJPR* 20 (1986): 70. Craig further argues that Ockham's view cannot be understood properly without reference to counterfactuals. Craig defines soft facts as a past or present event or actuality that is counterfactually dependent upon some future event or actuality in such a way that the earlier event or actuality is a consequence of which the latter event or actuality is the condition. If some future event is other than it will be, then the past facts would as a consequence have to be different than what they were. A hard fact is not so dependent. No matter how future conditions vary, a hard fact cannot be different than it was. See ibid., 83–85.

gently true because those propositions logically could be false. God could have acted otherwise such that he would have known differently. Thus, future contingent propositions about God's future actions are soft facts that do not yet possess accidental necessity. As a result, the truth value of these propositions is contingent upon God's future action. Therefore, God knows those propositions as contingent rather than as accidentally necessary. Further, God could possess power over the past. If God would have acted differently, then he would have known differently. In different possible situations, God could act otherwise and foreknow that he will act otherwise. He will in fact not act differently than what his foreknowledge states, but this is no loss of freedom. It is only a restraint in God's ability to do otherwise. Thus, it could be argued that divine freedom escapes the implications of God's foreknowledge of the future. Though he foreknows what he will do, God remains free in the libertarian sense because he logically can do otherwise.

Divine Freedom and the Ockhamist Solution

The Ockhamist Solution has deficiencies that demonstrate that it is not a viable solution for solving the problem of foreknowledge and divine freedom. The most glaring issue with Ockham's view is that Ockham provides no answer to how God knows the truth of these contingent, future based propositions. These propositions about the future are contingent; therefore, they logically can be different according to Ockham so that the content of God's foreknowledge is different. God did not have to know them. Ockham, however, does not explain how it is that these propositions can be different such that the content of God's foreknowledge is different. Further, Ockham holds that all propositions have a truth value that is now unchangeable by God or anyone else. If contingent propositions about the future must have a truth value and that truth value cannot be changed by anyone or anything, then by what means could the truth value of these propositions be different? Without such a means, the content of God's foreknowledge does not seem to be contingent such that it could have been different. God's foreknowledge is what it is because future contingent propositions simply possess their truth value in a brute fashion. These implications raise serious problems for the Ockhamist position and its defense of libertarian freedom. If there is no means to make future-contingent propositions differ in their truth value, then the events they specify cannot differ. They must occur. Thus, no agent, not even God, could do other than what these propositions state.

This consequence appears to make such future contingent propositions necessarily true rather than contingently true since they are unable to be different by any means. No metaphysical manner exists in which these propositions can ever lack a truth value or possess a value different from the one they already possess. If these propositions about the future are contingent as Ockham claims, then their truth value must be relative. This raises a serious problem for Ockham's theory. If the truth value of future contingent propositions can be made different, then God appears to be either subject to change or fallible in his knowledge.[23] Of course, Ockham rejects these claims. According to Ockham, God's knowledge cannot be fallible; therefore, it cannot be made different from what it is. Further, Ockham believes that God is not subject to change, so his knowledge cannot be made different. As a result, no proposition can be made different in its truth value it seems. If future contingent propositions cannot be made different in their truth value, then the content of God's foreknowledge cannot be different from what it is since nothing can make it different. If God's foreknowledge cannot be different, then the claim that God's knowledge of the future is contingent is false.

These conclusions are particularly troubling for the divine choices and actions. If all future contingent propositions have an unchanging truth value, then those propositions concerning the divine choices and actions have an unchanging truth value. If there is nothing that can make the truth values of these propositions different, then these propositions about the divine actions cannot be made different. Further, these propositions possess their truth values logically prior to any of God's choices, and God knows them as true logically prior to his acting. Since God cannot act contrary to what he knows is true and neither he nor anything else can make the claims about his future actions be different, then God's choices and actions cannot be different. If God were to do other than what he knows is true, then he would be either fallible in his knowledge or subject to change in what he knows.

If this is the case, all of God's actions, including his choice of what to create, must be what they are since the truth value of those propositions regarding the divine actions cannot be different. Nothing can make them different. If the content of the divine foreknowledge and the truth values of propositions regarding the divine choices cannot be different, then logical fatalism follows. God may not act in any other way since nothing allows for his actions to be contingent. God knows all truths by nature, and nothing can affect those truths such that they are different. Consequently, God must act according to the truth of those propositions about the divine choices and ac-

---

23 Adams, *William Ockham*, 1146–1147. See also William of Ockham, *Predestination*, 50.

tions since those are the only truths possible. Since logical fatalism is not an acceptable outcome, Ockham's theory must be rejected.

The various theories that attempt to describe the Hard-Soft Fact Distinction also have severe difficulties. These difficulties cause such a collapse in the Hard-Soft Fact Distinction that it cannot be applied to God's foreknowledge, even his foreknowledge of his own future actions. John Martin Fischer argues that Adams's account does not supply a viable definition of the statement "a necessary condition of the truth of P" in her definition of a soft fact. This claim can be interpreted three ways. First, it could be interpreted as P entails Q where Q is the logical consequence of P. For example, if $2+2=4$, then $22+22=44$. The antecedent implies the consequent, and the consequent implies the antecedent. Second, it can be interpreted as P materially implies Q where Q is implied by P but P is not implied by Q. For example, if a moon exists, then a planet exists. The antecedent implies the consequent, but the consequent does not imply the antecedent. Some planets do not have moons. Third, it may be interpreted as Q is a necessary condition for P if and only if P would not be true or have been true if Q were not true or had not been true. For example, oxygen is a necessary condition for the existence of fire. Fischer notes that the problem with all of these interpretations is that they do not allow any proposition to express a hard fact. Any past tense proposition will entail all other propositions, even future tense propositions. Thus, a statement such as "Smith existed at t_1" will entail that Smith does not exist for the first time at t_2 where t_1 is earlier than t_2. This proposition, like all past tense propositions, is then partially about t_2 and therefore soft, not hard.[24]

The same issue of a viable definition plagues the other Hard-Soft Fact theories as well. Hoffman and Rosenkrantz argue that hard facts are not about any future time relative to t. Such a fact cannot entail the obtaining of a state of affairs at some time later than t, and any fact that does entail a future event later than t is soft. However, David Widerker, who later rejected the Ockhamist Solution, argues that there are facts that entail a future fact later than t that are actually hard. An example of such a fact is a person informing another of his foreknown beliefs. Once the person informs someone of his foreknown belief, then that act of informing is a hard fact, and that hard fact entails a future fact later than t. Just because a proposition entails a state of affairs at a time future relative to t, this does not demonstrate that the state of affairs is contingent and a soft fact. Some future events are logically or metaphysically

---

24 John Martin Fischer, "Freedom and Foreknowledge," *PR* 92 (1983): 73–75. See Paul Helm, "Divine Foreknowledge and Facts," *CJP* 4 (1974): 311–312.

necessary. As a result, they are hard facts.[25] Hoffman and Rosenkrantz's theory is too broad in its hard-soft distinctions. Further, it is questionable that any proposition can be UR or URP since at some point all things must cease repeating. If there are no UR or URP propositions, then there can be no hard facts under Hoffman and Rosenkrantz's theory.

When looking at Freddoso's concept of immediate propositions, it is not obvious that there are such propositions. An immediate proposition is one that is true in all possible worlds that share the same history of present moments up to the present time. Such propositions are therefore hard and accidentally necessary. Do any possible worlds share the same history of present moments up to the present time? In every possible world, the content of God's foreknowledge is different, and that content exists at every present moment in that world. Thus, every present moment implies the truth and existence of that specific content of foreknowledge and the future events it states will occur. As a result, no worlds can share the same history of present moments due to this difference in the content of God's foreknowledge. Thus, neither immediate propositions nor hard facts exist.

Zemach and Widerker argue that hard facts are propositions that are necessary because they are shared by the set of worlds that are ontologically exact with the actual world. However, are there possible worlds that are ontologically exact? If the ontology of a possible world includes all the objects and states of affairs which comprise it, then no possible worlds are ontologically exact since they all contain a different set of objects and states of affairs. Should any object or state of affairs within the entire world be different, then one would have a different set of objects and states of affairs and a different possible world. If they were exact, then they would be the same world. For example, the content of God's foreknowledge is different in every possible world making no worlds ontologically exact. Since it is not obvious that possible worlds can be ontologically exact, it is not obvious that Zemach and Widerker's theory can support the concept of hard facts. Thus, their theory fails.

---

25 David Widerker, "Troubles with Ockhamism," *JP* 87 (1990): 466–468. Widerker elsewhere argues that the ability to remember a past fact shows that the past fact is a hard fact. One cannot remember something that is not fixed and settled. Such facts are hard, not soft. The same can be argued of any past fact of which an agent is informed by another agent. Once the agent informs another agent of his belief in what will occur, then that fact claim is a hard fact that is fixed and settled. That particular fact of informing is hard, and any fact contained within that hard fact is also hard. See David Widerker, "Why God's Beliefs are Not Hard-Type Soft Facts," *RS* 38 (2002): 84. John Martin Fischer also argues that belief is a hard property that can be possessed by a soft fact. This hard property cannot be changed by any agent's action such that God would not have possessed them. Thus, God's beliefs and remembrances are fixed. See Fischer's "Hard-Type Soft Facts," *PR* 94 (1986): 596–599.

Another major issue with the Hard-Soft Fact Distinction regards the freedom of actions. Even if it is possible that God and other agents act differently across different possible worlds, God and other agents still could not act differently *within* any one world. Propositions contained within each and every possible world as well as the actual world possess a specific truth value within those worlds. While some of those propositions may possess a different truth value in other possible worlds, they cannot possess a different truth value within the world of which they are a part. Once a specific world with its specific set of propositional truths obtains, then events cannot logically be different from what that set of propositional truths states. Once a possible world with its set of propositions obtains, all of those propositions would become hard facts. As a result, God and other agents could act only according to the truths of the possible world that has obtained. They could not do otherwise and would be determined. As a result, God and other agents may be libertarianly free *across* worlds but it does not appear that they can be libertarianly free *within* worlds.

If libertarian freedom is the only true freedom as the Ockhamist claims, then no choices and actions within worlds, including God's, can be free. All facts within worlds are hard and necessary, since they could only be soft and contingent across worlds. The Ockhamist must conclude then that either God's actions within possible worlds are not free or that libertarian freedom is not the only viable form of freedom. This problem is exacerbated if there is no means for determining which possible world obtains. If God is not able to determine which world and set of propositions obtains, then logical fatalism occurs since there is only one logically possible world.

The Hard-Soft Fact Distinction poses three other general problems. The first, noted by William Hasker, is that the Hard-Soft Fact Distinction is inadequate. Instead, Hasker makes a distinction between HARD/SOFT facts and hard/soft facts. The former are those propositions for which it is or is not possible that anyone should be able to make their truth value different. The latter are those that are or are not about the past. Hasker notes that just because a fact is hard does not mean that it is HARD, and just because a fact is soft does not mean that it is SOFT. There are hard facts that are SOFT because an agent could have made those facts false, such as *Jones mowed his lawn*. Further, there could be soft facts that, though they are not about the past, could still be HARD in that no one can make their truth value be different, such as *God will exist*. Also, all HARD facts are closed under entailment, like logic, but all hard facts are not.²⁶ The question that remains is whether or not the truth values of what God foreknows can be different and SOFT, and the Ockhamist Solution has not demonstrated that they can.

John Shook presents a second general problem with the Hard-Soft Fact Distinction. Shook argues that the Hard-Soft Fact Distinction notes which of God's beliefs are justified and which are not. When God's beliefs are justified, what God believes is true, God believes it to be true, and he has a justified reason for believing it to be true. According to Shook, hard facts are justified while soft facts are not. Shook maintains, however, that Ockhamists fail to consider that God is/has justification for all of his beliefs. In fact, he has that justification irrespective of other agents' considerations or situations since he possesses justification prior to the existence of any agent or situation. Since it is highly unlikely that any Ockhamist, or theist for that matter, will reject the claim that God has justified knowledge, then it must be concluded that the hard/soft fact distinction collapses. If God is justified, then anything that he knows must be a hard fact because it is justified. The only way God's belief could be soft is if God did not have justification, but without justification he could and would not know in the first place. If God has foreknowledge, then those foreknown beliefs must be hard facts and libertarian freedom is impossible.²⁷ The same then applies to God's foreknowledge of his own actions. If God has justified beliefs about his own future choices, then that knowledge is a hard fact. Since all propositions about any divine action have a truth value, they are justified and hard. As a result, it is impossible that God have alternate possibilities that are open to him in any situation, even creation. This conclusion not only denies God libertarian freedom but also makes him logically fated.

---

26 William Hasker, "Hard Facts and Theological Fatalism," *Nous* 22 (1988): 422–423. Hasker also argues that the reason that propositions about what God believed at a past time about a future event cannot be hard is because the agent designated by the name *God* implies infallibility. Since God cannot hold a false belief in any possible world, God's beliefs are not hard facts whose truth value can be different but are HARD. Hasker then argues that the same does not hold for the name *Yahweh*. Taken as a connotative name without any conceptual import, any proposed past tense proposition about a future event regarding the belief of the agent Yahweh will be either immediate or a hard fact. However, the proposition *if Yahweh exists, then Yahweh is God* is true in every possible world by metaphysical entailment. It is a HARD fact, and any proposition that it entails is also HARD. Therefore, any past tense proposition about a future event and using the agent name Yahweh or God, such as *Yahweh/God believed that Jones will mow his lawn*, will be both hard and HARD. Therefore, any proposition about the future that is foreknown by God cannot be soft or SOFT. Thus, the Hard-Soft Fact distinction must be false. See ibid., 429–431.

27 John Shook, "God's Divinely Justified Knowledge is Incompatible with Human Free Will," *Forum Philosophicum: International Journal for Philosophy* 15 (2010): 141–159.

Linda Zagzebski raises the third general problem with the Hard-Soft Fact Distinction. Zagzebski has no doubt that with enough time and counterexamples, a satisfactory formulation of hard and soft facts can be established; however, she sees no reason to think that it provides a real rather than nominal distinction between facts. According to Zagzebski, the Hard-Soft Fact Distinction is really no distinction at all. Instead, it is more like a gimmick used to avoid abandoning a cherished position.[28] The criticisms provided in the previous paragraphs support this argument. If all past tense propositions entail contingent future tense propositions, then there can be no distinction between facts. If immediate propositions are no different from non-immediate propositions, then no distinction between facts can be made. If no worlds are ontologically exact, then the distinction between facts is nominal, not real. If divine infallibility makes the truth of God's foreknowledge impossible to be different, then no distinction can be made. If all of God's foreknown beliefs are justified, then any distinction in facts collapses. Thus, the Hard-Soft Fact Distinction is inconsequential and cannot be an adequate solution to the problem of foreknowledge and divine freedom.

The notion of counterfactual power over the past also has problems. Linda Zagzebski explains that there are three possible explanations of this power over the past. The first explanation is that the agent can causally change the past, which is incoherent. The second is that the agent can bring it about that the past is different from what it was. Again, this view must be false since it implies that backwards causation actually happens. Even if such causation is possible, it is not evident that it occurs in this world. The third explanation is that an agent can act such that the past would have been different. However, if God's belief is not really in the past as supporters of atemporalism hold, then an agent causing God's belief is not a case of backwards causation, and counterfactual power is not needed. If God's belief is past as the temporalist holds, then counterfactual power is also ruled out as incoherent. If the future is not actual and real, then there can be no power of any kind over the past.[29] Thus, no agent can possess counterfactual power over the past, not even God.

As William Hasker points out, Plantinga's position is inconsistent regarding not only Zagzebski's claims but also the libertarian freedom Plantinga wishes to defend. Hasker notes that Plantinga is not claiming that if God has always believed *A* that it is in an agent's power to bring it about that God has not always believed *A*. Rather, if God has always believed *A*, then it is in an

---

28 Zagzebski, *Dilemma of Freedom and Foreknowledge*, 74–75. As a result, Zagzebski believes the argument to be *ad hoc*.

29 Ibid., 80–82. Zagzebski's argument seems to imply that counterfactual power over the past is just a disguised form of backwards causation.

The Ockhamist Solution

agent's power to do something such that if he *were* to do it, then God *would* not have believed A. This is counterfactual power over the past, not power to bring about the past.[30] Hasker, however, argues that the distinction between these two types of powers collapses based on his Power Entailment Principle (PEP). It is as follows:

> (PEP3) If (a) it is within S's power to bring it about that "*P*" is true and (b) it is within S's power to bring it about that "*P*" is false and (c) "*P*" entails "*Q*" and "*not-P*" entails "*not-Q*", then it is within S's power to bring it about that "*Q*" is true.

This PEP shows that an agent has the power to do something that would have brought it about that God does not hold a belief he did hold (i.e. change the past). If it is within an agent's power to bring about his action and his (not) acting entails what God believes, then an agent has the power to bring about what God believes.[31] According to Hasker, what Plantinga is actually stating is that an agent has the ability of backwards causation rather than a counterfactual power over the past. An agent can actually bring about something that changes what has already obtained, but no one can change the past once it has obtained. Not even God can utilize backwards causation to affect what he believed in the past. If no agent, not even God, can do this, then no one, not even God, can affect divine foreknowledge. Thus, everything is fixed and must unfold according to that knowledge, even the foreknown choices and actions of the divine life. Logical fatalism is implied for the divine choices because nothing and no one can make them other than what they are.

Plantinga, following in the footsteps of Ockham, has claimed that the truth value of the divine beliefs cannot actually be changed, which compounds the logical fatalism conclusion. If the divine beliefs, particularly those concerning divine action, cannot actually be changed and be different, then what power does an agent, like God, have over the past? If the truth value of the divine beliefs is immutable, then appealing to some sort of power that an agent supposedly possesses but does not and cannot ever express achieves nothing. The content of the divine foreknowledge remains what it is, its truth value and content cannot be different, and an agent, like God, cannot alter what will transpire according to that foreknowledge. Even if God does possess the

---

30 Hasker, *God, Time, and Knowledge*, 102. See Widerker, "Troubles with Ockhamism," 470–471.

31 Ibid., 106–111. Note that *bring about* is not necessarily causal but can be non-causally consequential. See also Thomas Talbott, "On Divine Foreknowledge and Bringing About the Past," *PPR* 46 (1986): 455–469, and Zagzebski, *Dilemma of Freedom and Foreknowledge*, 78.

power to act differently so that he would have believed differently, he cannot express that power and change his beliefs. God's beliefs regarding his own future choices and actions must have an unchanging and infallibly known truth value; therefore, it is not possible that God would have believed differently since he cannot act differently than what his beliefs indicate. God remains determined in all of his choices which leads to logical fatalism. The notion of power over the past fails to make God a free being.[32]

Conclusion

I have examined all of the various nuances of the Ockhamist Solution and found them wanting as a solution to the problem of foreknowledge and divine freedom. Ockham's own solution collapses, for he cannot adequately explain how God's knowledge about the future is contingent and could be different. As a result, his position leads to fatalism of the divine choices. The Hard-Soft Fact Distinction fails since it can make neither a real nor adequate distinction between necessary and contingent facts as they pertain to divine foreknowledge. Further, the justification of God's knowledge also interferes with the contingency of what he knows. Since there are true propositions concerning everything that God will do, God must know them and be completely justified in what he knows. Unless these propositions can be different in their truth value, all God's actions are necessary which leads to fatalism. Lastly, an agent's power over the past is either backwards causation, which is absurd, or an innocuous notion with no real effect. God cannot express the power to change what he knows; therefore, the content of his knowledge cannot be different than what it is. Thus, God's knowledge of his own choices and actions cannot be different, and he cannot act otherwise in any situation, leading to fatalism.

I conclude then that the Ockhamist Solution cannot be successfully applied to God's foreknowledge of his own future choices and actions. The problem of fatalism for the divine choices and actions pervades this solution. Also, libertarian freedom, the only type of freedom this position will accept, is lost for the divine choices and actions, leaving God not free. As a result, the Ockhamist Solution fails to uphold the first criterion for a successful solution to the problem of foreknowledge and divine freedom and is rejected as a satisfactory position.

---

32 David Widerker labels such power as innocuous. See Widerker, "Troubles with Ockhamism," 470–471.

Chapter 6

The Atemporal Solution

The final chapter of this study focuses on the Atemporal Solution as a possible means to resolving the problem of foreknowledge and divine freedom. There are a variety of atemporal views, and the view one holds affects how one understands God's knowledge of the future. In the first section of this chapter, I explicate those different facets of the atemporal position. In the second section, I explicate an argument raised against the viability of the Atemporal Solution. I conclude that while certain interpretations of the Atemporalist Solution do not avoid this criticism and do not solve the problem of foreknowledge and divine freedom, the logical moments model does. In conjunction with the logical moments model, I then provide an account of the Thomistic model of atemporal divine freedom. Lastly, I defend this model against various criticisms. I conclude that this version of the Atemporal Solution succeeds in solving the problem of foreknowledge and divine freedom and should be adopted.

Atemporalism

The Atemporal Solution has a long and impressive pedigree. Though it has fallen on hard times in contemporary philosophy and theology, the Atemporal Solution has existed for around fifteen hundred years and is a pillar of medieval philosophy and theology. This view of divine foreknowledge was first formally expressed in the writings of Boethius. When addressing the issue of foreknowledge and free will, Boethius first notes that it does not matter whether the future is determined by what is foreknown or that what is to happen in the future determines what is foreknown. Either way, claims about the future have a determinate truth value. Boethius believes that this implication can be seen in the example of a man who is sitting. If a man is sitting, then the fact that he is sitting is true and cannot now be otherwise. Further, if it is true to claim that the man is sitting because he is sitting, then it is necessary that he is sitting. Both claims involve necessity according to Boethius. In the former, the claim is necessary because the act of sitting is actual; in the latter, the act of sitting is necessary because the claim, which is grounded by the act, is true. Boethius then applies this implication to the problem of human freedom and foreknowledge. According to Boethius, both claims share a common necessity regardless of what causes the necessity. Whether God's knowledge implies the agent's act or the agent's act is actual such that God knows it, freedom is impossible because the agent's act cannot be otherwise. For Boethius, both positions imply determinism. Boethius also notes that what is known is certain and must be. To think that something is the case when it is not or will not be the case is either opinion or a false belief, but it is not knowledge. If the belief is not determinate in its truth value, then it cannot be foreknown.[1]

For Boethius, God is a knower who does not hold either opinion or false belief. Since Boethius operates with a correspondence theory of truth, God's knowledge corresponds to something in reality. Boethius asks how God can foreknow things that are contingent. To what do these foreknown contingent propositions correspond? They do not appear to correspond to anything since the objects and events they indicate do not yet exist. As a result, either God cannot know claims about the contingent future since those claims correspond to nothing or he can only speculate about the contingent future, which does not comprise real knowledge. Boethius accepts neither position.[2]

How then is the compatibility of foreknowledge with free will to be explained? Boethius argues that people want to judge God's wisdom by their own methods of knowledge. Since people cannot see how it is possible to foreknow a contingent action, then they think that God cannot know it either; however, God's method of knowledge is above man's level. In fact, it is quite possible that God utilizes different methods of knowing than humans do.[3] How then does God know the future? Boethius replies with his famous

---

[1] Boethius, *The Consolation of Philosophy*, rev. ed., trans. Victor Watts (Penguin, 1999), 120–121.

[2] Michael Robinson, *Eternity and Freedom* (University Press of America, 1995), 30–31.

[3] Boethius, *Consolation of Philosophy*, 126–128, 130–131. Boethius states that everything that is known is comprehended not according to its nature but according to the ability to know of the knower. For example, one may use the abilities of sight, imagination, and reason to know things. The highest ability is knowledge of simple form for it encompasses the others without

definition of divine timelessness. Eternity is "the complete, simultaneous, and perfect possession of the whole of all of one's life or existence."[4] According to Boethius, God's timeless existence is completely non-temporal. It is not a temporal moment of any kind but completely timeless lacking temporal extension and temporal location.[5] As a result, all things in reality, including all temporal events, occur and are viewed by God in his timeless moment. He does not possess his life or "see" things piecemeal because that would require a temporal progression. He "sees" all things occurring in the temporal realm in one timeless moment. God is able to "see" future times and events in his one timeless moment rather than waiting for those events to unfold in time. By "seeing" them, he is able to know them.

Using this definition of timelessness, Boethius concludes that foreknowledge is neither God's determination of what will happen nor prevision of things that will happen. Instead, foreknowledge is knowledge of what is actual. It is looking at rather than seeing beforehand. In fact, God views all temporal things the same way that a human being views things, and this viewing does not confer any necessity beyond what human vision supplies: conditional necessity. An event is necessary on the condition that if it obtains then it obtains; it is not necessitated to obtain by God's knowledge or by any other fact of reality. For example, a man is not necessitated to walk or sit, but if he does sit, it is necessary that he sits since his sitting is now actual. God's knowledge works the same way. He "sees" what is already occurring rather than knowing a fact before it has occurred.[6] Thus, a timeless God does not technically have foreknowledge but "present" knowledge of all facts, including human free choices.

Boethius avoids the removal of freedom by divine knowledge since God is merely "seeing" what an agent is currently and freely doing rather than that action being determined by God's will, God's knowledge, or by some prior fact in reality. As Brian Leftow argues, foreknowledge can only be a problem if it closes off options or limits the extent of an agent's power; however, God's

---

having to stoop to their method of knowing. For Boethius, God would certainly have the latter method but could utilize the other methods though he would not need to do so.

4 Ibid., 132–133. This definition would become a vital part of medieval philosophy and the definition of God. See Anselm, *Proslogion*, 19–21; idem, *Monologion*, 18–24; Aquinas, *Summa Theologica*, 1a.10.1 and 1a.10.2.

5 Alan Padgett, *God, Eternity, and the Nature of Time* (St. Martin's Press, 1992), 46; Stephen Davis, *The Logic and Nature of God* (Eerdmans, 1983), 9. There is some debate over whether or not timeless eternity could actually involve non-temporal extension and thus duration of some sort. See Eleonore Stump and Norman Kretzmann, "Eternity," *JP* 78 (1981): 429–458.

6 Boethius, *Consolation of Philosophy*, 134–136; Padgett, *God, Eternity, and the Nature of Time*, 45; Robinson, *Eternity and Freedom*, 32–33; Katherin Rogers, *Perfect Being Theology* (Edinburgh University Press, 2000), 84.

knowledge does not have this effect since it is possible that God knows something while perceiving or watching it as it happens. God's knowledge does not close off these choices either temporally or causally. Rather, they are produced and closed off by the agent acting in time. Leftow argues that temporal truths that are actual are also true in eternity because they are simultaneous with God's eternal state. No truth was true in eternity before the event because there is no time in eternity; eternity is not in the past or like the past. The obtaining of the event is what establishes the propositional truth of the event, but this does not imply that the event was true in any sense before the event occurred.[7] As a result, the agent is not determined by any truth regarding the action before he commits the action. He is completely free to act however he wishes to act.

This conclusion has several implications for God. Katherin Rogers argues that the causal flow of libertarian freedom necessitates that God obtain his knowledge by viewing human choices rather than possessing that knowledge essentially. As Rogers explains, there are three logical, not temporal, moments that define God's acquisition of knowledge. The first moment is the agent's free choice. In the second moment, God views that free choice. In the third moment, God possesses timeless knowledge of the free choice. All of these moments occur in one timeless instant but can be logically differentiated. Thus, the content of God's knowledge of the "future" is determined by human free action.[8]

An implication of this view is that God's knowledge depends upon the agent and his action. God cannot know the agent and his action without observing them. Some might object to God's knowledge being dependent in this way. Brian Leftow rejects this implication. He argues that agents act according to reasons based on character traits that produce desires. When one speaks of an agent, Leftow claims that one could refer to the way the agent is. He claims that people believe that the character trait is constitutive of the agent. The agent is the underlying character or nature and cannot be separated from it. Agents are not bare particulars. Rather, agents are intrinsically characterized in such a way that their character ensures how they would act.[9] Leftow claims that God could know the future prior to viewing it because he knows what character traits he has willed a person to have. As a result, he knows them so well that he can know how they would choose. Thus, he can string together

---

7 Brian Leftow, *Time and Eternity* (Cornell University Press, 1991), 250–253.

8 Rogers, *Perfect Being Theology*, 85–86. This position is similar to the Open Solution in that it asserts that the future is open to different possibilities and that free actions cannot be known until they are actualized and observed.

9 Leftow, *Time and Eternity*, 256–257.

the future based on all subsequent events and choices without being causally dependent on the actions of other agents for his knowledge. God does not will that the agent commit any particular act since the act is a causal outflow of the agent's character and nature, which is just the agent himself. Instead, it leaves it to the agent to determine his action even though God knows that the agent will act in a particular way.[10]

Leftow recognizes that this model implies a kind of determinism which libertarians are likely to reject. Character traits would have a causal effect on the agent such that they determine how an agent would act in any situation. To avoid this implication, Leftow's second proposal is that God has the ability to predict what agents will do with a very high probability. God knows the agent's nature and is able to predict, with fortunate impeccability, what the agent will do.[11] Thus, God need not be entirely dependent on creatures for his knowledge, but he is still dependent to some degree. Michael Robinson suggests that God is able to timelessly know a great many physical events since they are physically or causally necessary. This knowledge allows him further knowledge of what he may ontologically generate at a later temporal point. God knows creaturely events that occur at earlier temporal points, but he cannot know or anticipate some creaturely events in their entirety. God can only ontologically generate those parts of agents' lives that he knows are physically and causally necessary. Agents are left to self-determine the rest. All of this ontological generation occurs in a single eternal instant for God. Robinson believes that this proposal allows the agent options open to him which he has the power to bring about. However, God knows the free choice of agents and can sustain them in the one eternal instant.[12] These conceptions uphold a vibrant libertarian freedom and lead to a rejection of Rogers's conclusion that God's knowledge of the contingent future is specified by human action. Instead, human action only partially specifies God's knowledge of the future.

While Boethius assumes a particular model of timeless eternity, John Yates points out that there are two models of eternity. The first is a Platonic model in which time is a projection of a participation in eternity. God creates time, and the world temporally extends in accordance to the Platonic Form, or essence, of that world. Thus, the temporal world unrolls from the transcendent

---

10 Ibid., 261–263. Leftow refers to this position as Quasi-Molinism; however, he rejects the Molinist claim that there are truths about an agent's free action prior to God's creative activity. Since God decides what a person's character will be, such knowledge cannot be known prior to God's creative act.

11 Ibid., 263–265. See also Robinson, *Eternity and Freedom*, 202–204.

12 Robinson, *Eternity and Freedom*, 214–217.

rather than existing all at once and is determined by the transcendent. The second model of eternity is the Aristotelian model where all time is produced and embraced in an eternal now. Divine eternity is the mechanism that produces and grasps time all at once.[13] Boethius assumes the Aristotelian model as did classical theism, which states that God views all of time in his own unique vision. Many of these classical theists believed that God had a present relation with each moment of time that he views. Yates, however, argues that God does not have a relation with each moment of time or regard each moment as present to him. He argues that to do so assumes that God exists with all points of time simultaneously and knows them simultaneously. Using the Platonic model, Yates argues that the physical future does not exist for God to view because it has not yet become actual. Since the future does not exist, God cannot exist with future points of time and know them as present. Instead, God's knowledge of the temporal world must come from the divine ideas, which are the essences of worlds and objects. God does not view time or future non-existent objects because he cannot. All that God can view are his ideas and what they convey about the temporal world. God has no direct relation to the temporal world itself or to objects within time; he only has a relation to his own essence through which the essence of the temporal world and its objects are known to him.[14]

Yates further argues that the Platonic model rules out predetermination because it involves temporal relations which a timeless God does not have. He also argues that God's act of knowledge does not imply determinism. While it is necessary that God possess knowledge of the creation, this necessary possession does not imply the necessity of the creation. The latter is contingent. Instead, Yates argues that God causally affects human choices in a timeless manner. God is the eternal cause of all things. Further, there are ontologically different levels of causation such that God causes the existence of all things and sustains them. The creation, however, is left to act within the being and potentiality that it has received from God. God sustains but does not compete with other causes. All things act in dependence upon God but also express their own causal powers. Since God's causation does not precede

---

13 John Yates, *The Timelessness of God* (University Press of America, 1990), 52–53.

14 Robinson, *Eternity and Freedom*, 197–226, 232–233. Robinson believes that Boethius, Anselm, and Aquinas hold that God views time via the divine ideas, but he rejects the Platonic understanding. God's ideas are the means by which he views, not the thing he views. See Robinson, *Eternity and Freedom*, 38–42, 48–56; Anselm, *De concordia praescientiae et praedestinationis et gratiae dei cum libero arbitrio*, 1.5 and 3.1, trans. and ed. Jasper Hopkins and Herbert Richardson, in *Anselm of Canterbury*, vol. 2 (Edwin Mellon Press, 1976); Aquinas, *Summa Theologica*, 1a.14 and *Truth* 1.2.12.

temporal causation, God's sustaining cause and man's acting cause are concurrent with each other. Thus, no determination is implied.[15]

Yates's view, however, does not seem to rule out determinism of human action. First, if God is the cause of all things, then agents within creation do not seem to be left to cause other things. If they were, then God would not be the cause of something. Even if God is the sustaining cause of all things, this would still mean that he is not the direct cause of some things. Second, even if God is not the cause of an agent's actions, those actions must still occur in accordance with the essence of the created world. The essence, or Platonic Form, of the created world implies that certain events must occur because the created world participates with and is a projection of that essence; therefore, the essence of the created world determines all agent action in the created world. Thus, Yates's claim that the Platonic model avoids determinism is incorrect. This conclusion does not imply that the view is false. It only implies that Yates's position must support compatibilist human freedom rather than libertarian human freedom.

Assessment of the Atemporal Solution

Having examined the various interpretations of the Atemporal Solution, an examination of the implications of this view on divine freedom is in order. Does the atemporal view provide an appropriate model for understanding the divine freedom and resolving the problem of divine freedom and divine foreknowledge? Certain interpretations of this view are not appropriate models for solving the problem and thus should be rejected. The logical moments model, however, does provide an adequate solution to the problem of foreknowledge and divine freedom. In this section, I demonstrate how the logical moments model of the Atemporal Solution overcomes the problem of foreknowledge and divine freedom.

Implications for Divine Freedom

Some have argued that the Atemporal Solution to the problem of foreknowledge and human freedom is flawed and fails. If the position does fail, then such a failure would deal a serious blow to the hope of resolving the prob-

---

15 Yates, *The Timelessness of God*, 237, 241–268; Padgett, *God, Eternity, and the Nature of Time*, 57–59; Robinson, *Eternity and Freedom*, 238. See also W. Matthews Grant, "Can a Libertarian Hold that Our Free Acts are Caused by God?" *FP* 27 (2010): 22–44; Robert Koons, "Dual Agency: A Thomistic Account of Divine Providence and Human Freedom," *PC* 4 (2002): 397–410; Hugh McCann, "Divine Sovereignty and the Freedom of the Will," *FP* 12 (1995): 582–598.

lem of foreknowledge and divine freedom. Linda Zagzebski illustrates this critique in what she calls the timeless knowledge dilemma. First, God is claimed to be infallible in what he knows. Second, God timelessly believes that an agent will do S at t_3. Third, the agent is asserted to be free to refrain from doing S at t_3. However, the agent cannot be free to refrain from doing S at t_3 given the previous claims. In other words, God's timeless state implies that an agent is unable to change what God timelessly believes. Since what God believes is infallible, the agent seems unable to refrain from doing what God timelessly knows he will do.[16] Paul Helm argues along these same lines. He states that a timeless God cannot know "beforehand," but from a temporal agent's perspective, it can be said that God knew "beforehand." What God knows "beforehand" was true yesterday, and that is both in the past and necessary. As a result, what God knows is also past and necessary, so freedom is eliminated. Helm further states that what God knows "beforehand" is necessary because it is actual. Nothing can happen to change God's state of knowledge since it is impossible to change God's timeless state. If it could be changed, then God would not be timeless. Thus, it is impossible that God believes something different.[17]

A form of Zagzebski's and Helm's argument could also be applied to God. God is infallible, and he also timelessly believes that he will effect S at t_3, such as the parting of the Red Sea for the Israelites. Given these two claims, God does not seem to be free to refrain from effecting S at t_3. God's infallible and timeless state of belief thus implies that he must act according to what he infallibly and timelessly believes he will do. What God knows in his timeless state is infallible and must take place; therefore, God cannot refrain or act differently from what he timelessly knows he will do. This conclusion is true if God knows his own act of will in the moment logically prior to enacting it. As a result, God cannot be free in the libertarian sense when it comes to his actions within worlds. He could only be free in the compatibilist sense; however, divine compatibilist freedom was rejected in chapter two, and such freedom would eliminate the need for timeless vision of the future in the first place. If God knows the future by nature, then he does not need to view it in order to know it. Thus, it seems that God cannot be free regarding his actions within possible worlds, such as parting the Red Sea, in the atemporal view. One then must reject this view as a resolution to the problem of foreknowledge and divine freedom.

---

16 Zagzebski, *The Dilemma of Freedom and Foreknowledge*, 61.
17 Helm, *Eternal God*, 101, 105–106. See also Paul Helm, "Timelessness and Foreknowledge," *Mind* 84 (1975): 516–527.

The Atemporal Solution

The problems this critique implies are serious and have a direct connection to several of the proposed interpretation of the atemporal position. First, these problems arise in connection with an interpretation of divine freedom from Yates's Platonic perspective. The Platonic perspective, if applied to God, would imply that God knows what he will do by viewing himself and how he acts. The way that God views himself and his action is by viewing the idea he has of himself the same way that he views the world by viewing the idea he has of it. In this manner, God is able to know his own choices logically prior to choosing, just as he is able to know all temporal events of the world logically prior to creating them. This knowledge of the divine self is infallible and timelessly immutable such that it cannot be different.

Such a Platonic view, however, implies that the divine life and its actions are already determined by the divine idea of the divine nature and that all divine action must correspond with that idea. As a result, God cannot be libertarianly free if he must act according to a predetermined idea about himself that necessarily exists within the divine mind. In fact, such a view implies natural necessity and logical fatalism since all divine action and all of reality is determined by his idea of himself. Non-actualized possibility in such a view of the divine knowledge and freedom is impossible. Since Yates's view implies fatalism, God seems to lack freedom entirely. The claim that God possesses an idea concerning the divine nature that determines how he would act must be rejected. God may have an idea of himself, but that idea cannot determine how God would act. Given these implications, one must reject Yates's version of the atemporal position as an acceptable solution to the problem of foreknowledge and divine freedom. The consequence of this rejection, however, is that God ultimately does not know of his own act of will and its consequence logically prior to actualizing his will.

These same concerns about divine freedom and atemporalism arise in Leftow's appeal to character as a means to know the future. Applied to God, Leftow's theory implies that God can deduce all divine action from the divine character since all action flows from an agent's character. In God's case, he is the divine character. If God possesses a character by which he can deduce all his actions, then the divine character determines all divine action, even God's choice of a world to create. Since God is a perfectly good being, then one may conclude that God also has an essential character which directs his action. God's perfectly good nature and essential character determines exactly how he will act. God also infallibly knows of this implication of the divine nature and timelessly believes it. Logical fatalism follows from this position. God cannot do other than what his essential divine character determines him to do since the divine nature determines such action. To avoid this implication, one must reject that the divine character completely determines divine action. Leftow's appeal to character is clearly not a suitable solution to the problem of foreknowledge and divine freedom. Subsequently, Leftow's position faces the same consequence as the rejection of Yates's position: that God does not know of his act of will logically prior to willing it.

After rejecting both Yates's and Leftow's positions, one is left with Roger's logical moments position. In this position, God's timeless existence can be conceptualized as a series of logical moments rather than temporal moments. In the first moment, God exists in his essential state with his essential and natural knowledge. This knowledge includes all knowledge about what is possible and logically deducible. In the second moment, God actualizes an act of will. In the third moment, God possesses his free knowledge of what he wills and its effects. The logical moments framework escapes fatalism and affirms libertarian freedom by asserting that God's act of will is not necessitated by any law of logic or fact of nature.

Like the Open Solution, the logical moments framework rejects the claim that God's knowledge of his act of will is logically prior to actualizing that act of will. Knowledge of the divine choice is not in the first logical moment as part of God's essential natural knowledge. If this were the case, then that knowledge would be based in either a law of logic or a fact of the divine nature and would be determined. Since God's choice must not be determined but libertarianly free, then his knowledge of that choice cannot be based in a law of logic or a fact about the divine nature. God, therefore, cannot have natural knowledge of his act of will logically prior to his actualization of that act of will. The logical moments framework embraces the position that God does not possess knowledge of what his act of will is and its effects in the first logical moment. Instead, he possesses such knowledge in the third logical moment. As a result, the logical moments framework is able to avoid the threat of fatalism since the content of God's knowledge is not determined. In this logical moment, nothing determines God's choice. It is libertarianly free. God faces open possibilities regarding how he may act. Thus, the logical moments framework appears to be an acceptable ground for solving the problem of foreknowledge and divine freedom because it upholds the first criterion of a successful solution: the rejection of fatalism. Further, because God's timeless state of knowledge is concurrent with his free acting, there is no concern that God cannot change his timeless state of knowledge. His free choice determines that timeless state of knowing.

An Atemporal Understanding of Divine Freedom

Having determined that the logical moments framework is acceptable as a solution of the problem of foreknowledge and divine freedom, a demonstration of how the divine freedom operates within this atemporal position is in order. Demonstrating that the logical moments framework allows for libertarian freedom is one thing. Showing that it is coherent with a timelessly acting God is another thing. This position must also be shown to be consistent with the other criteria for a successful solution to the problem of foreknowledge and divine freedom. This position must allow for a perfectly good God to act freely and not by natural necessity. It must also be consistent with the theory of divine ideas as outlined in the first chapter. A successful solution to the problem of foreknowledge and divine freedom must be able to meet these requirements as well.

Fortunately, the logical moments view of the Atemporal Solution meets the requirements outlined in the preceding paragraph. Thomas Aquinas proposes in his writings an atemporal understanding of divine freedom. Aquinas first notes that a being that possesses a mind has an intellect. Subsequently, the presence of an intellect also implies the presence of a will. Intellectual beings are able to choose and act. Since God is a mind, he has an intellect and therefore has a will.[18] The conclusion then must be that God possesses a will that is able to choose and act. How exactly does God will and what may he will? Aquinas argues that God principally wills his essence or wills himself because God himself is the most supreme good to be sought; therefore, God's aim in acting is his own goodness. Aquinas asserts that this aim is essential to the divine nature for two reasons. First, God is his own aim essentially because he is essentially supremely good, and it is fitting that God should seek himself. Second, nothing outside of God himself can move him. If God is to be moved to act, he must be moved by himself alone. His act of willing essentially flows from his being. Thus, God's supremely good nature essentially moves him to seek himself. He is the ultimate end to be willed.[19]

Aquinas's position implies that God must necessarily actualize an act of will. He cannot exist without willing since his goodness is necessary and it necessarily moves him to act. The position also implies that what God wills is his own goodness, and he necessarily wills his own goodness. These im-

---

18 Aquinas, *Summa contra Gentiles*, 1.72.
19 Aquinas, *Summa contra Gentiles*, 1.74, 1.80; *Summa Theologica*, 1a.19.1; Leftow, *Time and Eternity*, 301–302.

plications raise two pressing questions. First, is God able to will things other than himself? The second question is more troubling. If God necessarily wills his own goodness, then is not divine freedom abandoned for he must will of necessity? Aquinas addresses these questions. Addressing the first question, Aquinas states that in willing himself God wills things other than himself. God wills the divine goodness, and all subsequent things are willed for that one end. Consequently, God wills all things, like people and animals, other than himself for the sake of himself.[20] As a result, all things exist as a means to the one supreme divine end: the divine goodness. They do not exist for their own separate ends but in order to achieve the essential aim of God's act of will. Thus, in seeking himself, God does create things different from himself.

In response to the second question, Aquinas claims that while God's act of will is absolutely necessary, what is willed is not absolutely necessary. God must actualize some act of will, but the content of that act of will is not necessary. Aquinas states that what is willed for the sake of an end is not necessary if the end can be satisfied without what is willed. Thus, the will can will anything that can satisfy the end which it seeks. Many things can satisfy the divine goodness, which is the end that God wills, and God can will many different things in order to satisfy that end. As a result, God is not necessitated to will certain things.[21] No necessary connection exists between what God wills and the end that he wills. The divine goodness does not imply that only a certain set of things can exist; therefore, God's will is not logically or naturally necessitated. This implication connects back with the answer to the first question considered. God wills for the sake of the divine end, but what is willed by God is not logically or naturally caused. No law of logic or fact of nature restricts what God wills or causes him to will in a certain manner. God's act of willing is caused, and that causation proceeds from the divine nature. The reason that what God wills is not caused is because it is for the sake of the divine end. Since there are many different means for achieving that end, what God wills cannot be necessary. It must be contingent.[22] As a result, what God wills does not necessarily flow from the necessary fact that he must will.

For Aquinas, the act of will and what is chosen by the act of will are two different things. The former is absolutely necessary but the latter is not. Thus, God retains libertarian freedom in that he may freely choose the content of his will. He may freely choose the means by which to satisfy the divine end. Aquinas demonstrates this difference in his appeal to the difference between

---

20 Aquinas, *Summa contra Gentiles*, 1.76.
21 Ibid., 1.81.
22 Ibid., 1.87; Leftow, *Time and Eternity*, 301–302.

absolute and hypothetical necessity. Absolute necessity is something that is necessary by logical implication. The laws of logic require that it be. On the other hand, hypothetical necessity is the supposition that while something obtains, it cannot be otherwise. Hypothetical objects could fail to exist, but once they do exist, it cannot be other than that they exist when they exist. That God produces an act of will is absolutely necessary. God's goodness necessarily moves him to act, and God's timeless existence must be fully actualized from all eternity. Thus, the divine act of will must necessarily be fully actualized from all eternity. On the other hand, what God wills is only hypothetically necessary.[23] Given the hypothetical statement that God is currently willing *A*, then it follows that he cannot currently be willing *not A*. Thus, what God wills is necessary by the supposition that he is currently willing it in his timeless state. Since the act is atemporally occurring, it cannot be other than what it "now" is. This does not mean that God's act of will logically could not have been otherwise. It only implies that it is "now" impossible for it to be different since the divine atemporal state cannot be changed. Thus, Aquinas concludes that while the willing of the divine end is absolutely necessary for God, he is not bound to will what he wills to achieve that end. God can obtain his end without the need of certain things. He does not of necessity need anything to achieve his end, so no specific means is absolutely necessary to achieve the necessary divine end.[24]

Finally, Aquinas notes that while God is perfectly good and it is impossible that he do what is evil, he is not determined to choose according to his perfect goodness. Instead, Aquinas asserts that God chooses from a multiplicity of good options over which the dictates of morality provide no necessary connection.[25] Aquinas concludes that God has free choice since what he wills is not absolutely necessary. He possesses will regarding his end, but he possesses free will in regards to the means to achieve that end. Thus, God does not will by nature but by the judgments of reason. God reasons according to his end determining the best means according to him for achieving his end. God then acts upon that reason.[26] Given this distinction between the divine act of will and what is willed, Aquinas preserves divine libertarian freedom and rejects determinism. Thus, he avoids the concerns of the second question.

A clearer picture of how the divine freedom functions within an atemporal existence has now emerged. God exists in his atemporal and immutable state of being. As a result of this state of being and by implication of the di-

---

23 Aquinas, *Summa Theologica*, 1a.19.3; *Summa contra Gentiles*, 1.83.
24 Ibid.
25 Aquinas, *Summa Theologica*, 1a.19.10.
26 Aquinas, *Summa contra Gentiles*, 1.86, 1.88.

vine goodness, God must eternally actualize an act of will. God is directed by his own nature to seek his own goodness, which is his aim or end in acting. While God must necessarily eternally actualize an act of will, what he wills is not absolutely necessary. All things exist for the sake of achieving the divine end. Since there is a multiplicity of things that can achieve the divine end, God is not logically or naturally necessitated to choose any one means to achieve this end. God is thus free in the libertarian sense to choose among the multiplicity of things in order to achieve the divine end. Since God is atemporal and must actualize an act of will, what God wills is also atemporally actualized. Since what God wills is "now" being willed, it is hypothetically necessary and cannot now be otherwise; therefore, God does not will by logical or natural necessity. God freely judges what is the best and the appropriate means by which to achieve his end. Thus, God does not act arbitrarily but for a reason: his goodness. This free act of will according to reason is fully actualized for all eternity in God's atemporal state.

This picture fits perfectly within the logical moments framework. Since one cannot use temporal moments to distinguish the events of God's act of willing, one must do so conceptually. Thus, God in his essential being possesses natural knowledge of all that is logically possible. The divine nature states that God must actualize an act of will due to his goodness and timelessness. Logically posterior to this logical moment, God actualizes his act of will. This act of will conceptually follows from the fact that God must actualize an act of will; however, what God wills remains free. Logically posterior to this second moment is God's free knowledge. This knowledge conceptually follows from God's act of will because God knows what he wills when he wills it. All of this obtains in one atemporal "now" rather than in temporal moments; therefore, God is now freely willing and knowing what he wills. God is not determined, and fatalism is not implied. Thus, the atemporal view that uses the logical moments model presents a coherent picture of the divine will.

Is this view compatible with divine goodness? Does this atemporal model allow for God to be free regarding his perfect goodness? As indicated in the criteria for a successful solution to the problem of foreknowledge and divine freedom, a successful solution avoids limiting God's act of will to just one possible way a perfectly good being can act. Fortunately, the logical moments framework in conjunction with the Thomistic position allows for God to remain free in relation to his perfect goodness in one sense. God is not free in regards to his perfect goodness in his end for which he acts.[27] Because God is

---

27 While God is not free in regards to the aim for which he acts, this position is compatible with God having secondary aims. This notion is seen most clearly in Aquinas's claim that

perfectly good, he must necessarily seek himself and his own goodness as his end for acting. God is free in regards to his perfect goodness in the means by which he wills to obtain his own goodness. Because God may select from a multiplicity of good things by which he may obtain his end, he is not determined to choose from only one available option. Thus, the logical moments framework is neither inimical to the demands of perfect goodness nor to the demands of divine freedom. It allows for both.

There is also the issue of the divine freedom as it relates to the theory of divine ideas and possible worlds. As noted in the first two chapters, the divine ideas serve as Platonic forms and the basis for all things that can exist. Among these divine ideas are possible worlds, and each world contains a specific set of divine actions that must occur in order for that world to obtain. If God wills to create a particular world, then it follows that he must also perform certain acts within that world in order for that world to obtain. This consequence appears to restrict God's freedom in most if not all of his acts. It also appears to make God temporal. How can the atemporal position outlined here address this challenge to the divine freedom from the divine ideas?

The atemporal position is not without defense, and proponents of this view could respond in several different ways. First, the atemporalist could note that the set of divine actions that belong to a particular world are not a set of individual actions that stem from their own independent and individual act of will at a certain time. If they were such actions, then God would certainly be determined in how he chooses and acts at certain times. According to the atemporal position, however, God is not in time; therefore, he does not act at certain times. If he does not act at certain times, then the divine actions within the world cannot be singular and individual. For the atemporalist, God has only one divine and timeless act of will, not individual acts of will spread across the temporal world. Second, the atemporalist position could note that all the divine actions spread across the temporal world are the multiple effects of the one timeless divine act of willing.[28] Paul Helm provides an analogy of this one divine act of will. Helm compares this act of divine willing to that of a person setting a thermostat. When setting the thermostat, one programs the thermostat in one act at one moment to engage and disengage the heating and cooling system at certain times. This one act of setting the thermostat thus has numerous temporally scattered effects.[29] The same can be

---

there are various means to achieving the divine end. God has other purposes than the glorification of himself, but all of these other purposes contribute to this primary aim.

28 See Aquinas, *Summa Theologica*, 1a.19.2; *Summa contra Gentiles*, 1.76.

29 Paul Helm, "Divine Timeless Eternity," in *God and Time*, ed. Gregory Ganssle (InterVarsity Press, 2001), 53–54.

said of God's one atemporal act of will. It is one act of will that causes numerous effects within the world rather than being separate, individual acts of will with separate, individual effects spread out across time. Rather than willing in piecemeal fashion, God wills all of his various actions, as well as all things, in one unifying act of will, and all effects proceed from that one act of will.

As a result, the atemporalist need not worry about the divine ideas determining divine action. Yes, a specific set of divine effects are required for a particular world to obtain, but God freely chooses to actualize that specific set of divine effects in his one atemporal act of will. While the divine idea requires certain effects to be actualized in order for a certain possible world to obtain, the divine idea does not possess causal power over God, forcing him to choose that world and its effects. Nothing in the world possesses causal power over God to force him to act as he does. All things, including the divine effects within the world, flow from and are determined by the free divine act of will. While the divine actions within the world are a necessary feature of that world, they are a contingent effect of the one atemporal act of divine will. As a result, an atemporal God is free regarding the implications of the divine ideas on his actions within the world. A Platonic model of timelessness is not incompatible with the divine ideas and divine freedom, but neither is an Aristotelian model of timelessness. God could create the entire temporal world with all of the divine actions it contains out of his one timeless and free choice using the divine idea as his exemplar. All of God's actions would still be free. As a result, the Atemporal Solution succeeds in meeting all of the criteria for a successful solution to the problem of foreknowledge and divine freedom. It avoids fatalism, it avoids natural necessity in relation to God's perfect goodness, and it is compatible with the theory of divine ideas and its implications.

Criticisms of the Atemporal Solution

Critics of the Atemporal Solution believe it creates potential problems for the divine being. They argue that such a view of God's relationship to the temporal future is impossible. They claim that the future does not actually exist; therefore, how can God view what does not exist temporally? Time would seem to be an illusion.[30] The same issue can be raised concerning God and his own life. How can God view his life when parts of his life seem to not yet exist,

---

30 See Davis, *Logic and the Nature of God*, 14–15, Kenny, *The God of the Philosophers*, 38–39, and Prior, *Papers on Time and Tense*, 43–44. They argue that physical existence, if not existence *simpliciter*, implies temporality because anything that begins to exist exists at a time.

particularly those actions that occur within the temporal world? If temporal situations do not yet exist, then God's response to those situations cannot exist either. God's response is not yet actual; therefore, it is not part of his life and cannot be timelessly viewed. Such a conclusion is also incompatible with the notion of timelessness itself. A timeless God cannot lack or gain any part of his life. If he did, then God would be subject to temporal change, which is impossible due to divine timelessness.

How then can God view temporal becoming and be related to time? This concern over time and God's relation to it appears to be overblown. The primary source of contention is the claim that God is not able to view the future since it does not yet exist. Subsequently, he cannot view his own choice since it does not yet exist for him to view. This contention seems to miss the point that all of time is actual and presently exists to God in his timeless state. Consequently, even God's act of will is actual and presently exists to God in his timeless state. Since these things are actual and do exist, then God's ability to view these things does not create an issue. This criticism appears to be based on a misunderstanding of the nature of eternity as well as the relation of eternity to time. Why cannot God view the future in his timeless eternal state? It is because the future does not exist. It has not come into being; therefore, God cannot view it. This understanding, however, treats timeless eternity as if it were temporal. To say that a timelessly eternal God cannot view the future because it does not yet exist implies that at some point God will be able to view the future, which is to treat God's existence as temporal rather than atemporal. No temporally later point exists at which God can view the future or even view his own choice(s).

As a result, this criticism also misunderstands how an atemporal God creates the entire temporal realm in one atemporal instant. He does not create it piecemeal. Since the entire temporal realm is actual and exists, it can be viewed. The same applies with the divine choice. God actualizes his choice of a world in one atemporal instant such that it exists, and he can view it. He does not temporally proceed from a state of not acting to a state of acting. As Aquinas states, God essentially moves to act though how he acts is a contingent matter. God is always eternally acting; therefore, his act is eternally before his gaze. All things, including future temporal events, are completely actualized in atemporal eternity. Temporal becoming is unnecessary in atemporal eternity. For God, however, this lack of temporal becoming does not imply that temporal things do not yet exist to be viewed by him. Further, God can always view the future via the divine idea of the actual world. Even if certain parts of the actual world do not materially or temporally exist,

God always knows of those parts in his eternal state via the Platonic form in his mind.

The relation of this atemporal divine state to time also need not imply that time is an illusion. From a human being's frame of reference, time flows and can be measured, but from God's frame of reference, all of time is instantaneous. Even the effects of the divine will are instantaneous to the divine life. This difference in frame of reference, rather than indicating that time is an illusion, merely indicates that God perceives the flow of time differently than human beings do. Human beings perceive time as flowing from one moment to another whereas God perceives the flow of temporal reality in one instantaneous moment. Thus, time exists, but it is perceived differently. God's atemporal existence also need not imply that it is impossible that God have a relation with time. God merely relates to time in a manner that is different from how a temporal being relates to time. As a result, divine atemporalism and God's ability to know both the temporal world and his own act of will is completely coherent.[31]

The logical moments framework has implications for divine omniscience that draw other criticisms. The first criticism is that God's knowledge is to some degree dependent on the creatures he creates. This issue can also be applied to God in that his knowledge is also dependent on his act of will. Some theists may balk at the idea of God being dependent on creatures for his knowledge. God is not dependent on anything or anyone outside of himself. While the issue of God's knowledge depending on creatures is contentious, there is no apparent reason to object to the concept that God's knowledge is dependent on his own act of will. Since the divine act of will originates with

---

31 The position outlined here is reliant upon a specific metaphysical theory of time. The A-theory of time defines time as a temporal becoming. Entities are spoken of as being past, present, or future, and those entities move and transform across a series of temporal points. The B-theory of time defines time as static existence. Entities are spoken of as being before or after other entities. There is no movement and transformation across a series of temporal points since all temporal points of time are equally real and simultaneous. The atemporal position is dependent on the B-theory of time since it argues that God's life is a static existence and that all times simultaneously exist before God in this state of existence. For more on the nature of time and God's relation to time, see J. M. E. McTaggart, "The Unreality of Time," *Mind* 17 (1908): 457–473; William Lane Craig, "The Tensed vs. Tenseless Theory of Time: A Watershed for the Conception of Divine Eternity," in *Questions of Time and Tense*, ed. Robin Le Poidevin (Clarendon Press, 1998), 221–250; William Lane Craig, *Time and Eternity: Exploring God's Relationship to Time* (Crossway, 2001); Garrett DeWeese, *God and the Nature of Time* (Ashgate, 2004); idem, "Atemporal, Sempiternal, or Omnitemporal: God's Temporal Mode of Being," in *God and Time: Essays on the Divine Nature*, ed. Gregory Ganssle and David Woodruff (Oxford University Press, 2002), 49–64; Gregory Ganssle, ed., *God and Time: Four Views* (InterVarsity, 2001); Pike, *God and Timelessness*; Helm, *Eternal God*; Leftow, *Time and Eternity*.

God, he is not dependent on anything external to his being. Therefore, God possessing such a dependence relation to himself is not a concern.

A second criticism of the logical moments framework is more difficult. Since the content of God's knowledge is dependent on something else, God in his state of natural knowledge seems to lack certain knowledge and must add such knowledge to himself. As the logical moments framework states, God knows either an agent's choice or his own choice only in the logical moment when he views it. He does not know it in the first logical moment since that is logically prior to his choice. That first moment contains only God's natural knowledge, and God's knowledge of both his act of will and the world he has willed are not natural or essential to his being. Such a position implies that God makes his choice and possesses knowledge of it at moments two and three, both of which are logically posterior to God's natural state of being and knowledge. As a result, the content of God's act of will and his knowledge of the consequence of that act of will must be accidental to the divine being. Since such knowledge is accidental to the divine mind and divine being according to the logical moments theory, it must somehow have been obtained by the divine mind and the divine being. Even if this obtaining is actualized from all atemporal eternity such that there is no time at which it was gained, God must obtain it nonetheless.

While one may be tempted to conclude that God is not essentially omniscient or fully immutable based on this implication, this conclusion does not follow. God is only less than omniscient if he must add knowledge to his mind such that the amount of knowledge that he possesses increases; however, God does not lack any piece of knowledge. As the divine being and source of all things, he cannot fail to possess knowledge of what is true and what is false. While God essentially knows all truths, this does not mean that what he knows as true is always true. The truth value of the things that God knows could be different, and this is all that the logical moments position needs to imply. In the first logical moment, the content of God's knowledge is one way, and in the third logical moment, it is another. Since these two moments are simultaneous, the difference between the two is conceptual rather than temporal. At no time does God's knowledge change either in amount or content, though it could have been different in its truth value at certain logical moments. As a result, God is never without knowledge of all truths and falsehoods. God always and essentially knows all truths even if what he knows as true could have been otherwise. God's immutability also need not be questioned. Since God's act of willing is absolutely necessary, he must actualize that act of willing from all eternity. As a result, the effects of this act of willing are eternally actualized, and these effects include what God knows as true. No time exists at which the truth value of what God knows changes. The knowledge that God possesses he possesses from all eternity; therefore, God does not ever experience change even though his state of being in the first logical moment is different from his state of being in the third logical moment.

The position that some of God's knowledge is accidental has another major implication for the nature of the divine being and the divine omniscience. If the content of God's knowledge is accidental, then God possesses accidents as parts of his being. If the content of God's knowledge of the divine choices and their consequences is not essential to the divine nature, then this knowledge must be accidental and must be obtained. The same applies to God's act of will. How God acts is contingent and can be different and is accidental to the divine being. As a result, both the content of the divine knowledge and the specific act of the divine will are accidental to the divine being and are obtained. Since they are accidental and not essentially possessed, they appear to be constituent parts of the divine being. The traditional notion of divine simplicity is ruled out under this atemporal view.[32] Since God has accidents, he also has parts to which he is not identical. A simple being, however, cannot have parts separate and different from his being. It seems that God cannot be a simple being in the atemporal view.

Eleonore Stump, however, defends atemporalism against this criticism of divine simplicity and the divine freedom. Stump argues that this criticism is based on a particular definition of what an accident is. If one defines an accident as something that can come to be or be absent from a subject, then God has accidents and cannot be simple. Another definition, which she attributes to Aquinas, is that an accident is something that lacks metaphysical completeness. If something does not have subsistent being, then it is incomplete and accidental. God does not have any metaphysical incompleteness. Thus, something may be different than what it could be across possible worlds but still be metaphysically complete. Even though God's existence is variable across worlds, he still possesses complete being and simplicity.[33] Stump's position, however, draws two criticisms. First, her position depends on a particular definition of accidents which may not be correct, and Stump provides no reason to prefer her definition over another other than that it supports simplicity. Which definition of an accident is correct and whether or not God is a simple being are still unsettled. Second, Stump's view still implies that the

---

32 This claim goes back to Aquinas's contention that a simple being cannot have accidents. See Aquinas, *Summa Theologica* 1a.3.6.

33 Eleonore Stump, *Aquinas* (Routledge, 2003), 112–114.

divine being possesses parts that it need not possess. This implication comes from her statement that God's existence is variable across worlds. Thus, the divine existence is composed of parts, which are metaphysically complete of course. A simple being, however, cannot possess parts because such a being is completely identical to itself. If God possesses such parts, then it is false that God is a simple being in Stump's view. If Stump and others are content with the notion that a simple being can be comprised of metaphysically complete parts, a simple being may be a free being depending on one's definition of simplicity. Given this difference in opinion of the definition of simplicity, simplicity may not be compatible with a free atemporal God.

These are the implications of the atemporal position, but these consequences are not incompatible with the notion of God as a timelessly free agent. As previously stated, God must essentially act, but how he acts is not essential. Since God must essentially act in a non-essential way, God can timelessly bring about a state of being in which he is dependently and accidentally omniscient. How God chooses to act conditions God's omniscient knowledge. The accidental state in which God now resides conditions his immutability since that state is timelessly actual and cannot "now" be different. As a result, there is no apparent contradiction in holding to these consequences of the logical moments model and the atemporal view of divine freedom.

All proponents of the atemporal view do not agree with the position on divine freedom that has been presented here. Paul Helm objects to the Thomistic position on the ground that libertarian freedom and its liberty of indifference towards potential choices is detrimental to the understanding of God. Helm argues that God does not act by a necessity of nature, but he also does not have liberty of indifference to opt between equal alternatives. Rather, Helm claims that God is free to act in accordance with his supremely good nature without hindrance or coercion. For Helm, if God did not act in accordance with his nature, then God would not be worthy of worship. Helm sees no incoherence in the claim that God must choose some definite world and is still free.[34]

If God must create some definite world, then how is God free and not naturally necessitated? Helm argues that God has a logically contingent relation to the object of his will. According to Helm, God has at least one logically coherent alternative to what he chooses. God is also powerful enough to will and actualize that alternative; however, God has a good reason to prefer and

---

34 Helm, *Eternal God*, 173–174. This conclusion is because Helm supports compatibilist freedom.

choose one over the other. God contemplates these alternatives and rejects the ones that he does for this good reason in one timeless act, and changing what God wills is now impossible. According to Helm, this position does not depend on God having equally optimific alternatives from which to choose. If God did have such alternatives, Helm argues that God's act of will would be purely reasonless and based on whimsy. For Helm, God's freedom resides in the rationality of his choice rather than the ability to choose among alternatives.[35]

Helm's position raises an interesting question. Must God choose rationally and would this necessity harm the contingency of the divine choice? Helm responds that in a sense God does have to choose rationally because he is a rational being, but this language does not imply constraint. God freely acts according to who he is, and no explanation is possible except that what God chooses seems good to him.[36] Helm also states that it is true in a sense that God could have created an alternative universe since if it can be conceived, then it is possible. Since God can conceive of an alternative to this world, then that world is possible. While this alternative is conceptually possible and God possesses the power to actualize it, God would not necessarily actualize it. Indeed, the actual universe shows that he would not actualize other alternatives. While possibilities can be abstracted from God's will, they do not represent real possibilities and never did because of God's timeless state.[37] For Helm, divine alternatives are merely conceptual and not real in any sense. Further, the universe is not contingent because God is rationally indifferent towards it. Rather, it is contingent because its existence is not deducible from a set of logical truths. The universe is not necessitated by logic but by God's nature since God acts in accordance with his supremely good nature.[38] Since no divine choice has external constraint, God remains free on Helm's view.

Helm's strange view does not appear to be coherent. First, Helm claims that God does not act by a necessity of nature; yet, he also states that God necessarily acts in accordance with his supremely good nature. Helm even supports the claim that God must choose a certain world based on a reason that naturally flows from the divine nature. In fact, Helm claims that God's reason for acting is an extension of the divine character and his preference for certain things over others. Further, he sees divine alternatives as being purely conceptual and not really there for the taking. God could but would not create certain worlds because God's nature dictates that he not create

---

35 Ibid., 117–179.
36 Ibid., 181.
37 Ibid., 188–189.
38 Ibid., 187.

those worlds. If God's nature provides a reason, which implies that a specific world be chosen, then how is God not necessitated by nature? This position implies fatalism. Even if the dictates of the divine nature do not constitute an external constraint upon God, God still acts by natural necessity, which is a contradiction of Helm's earlier claim.

Helm may respond to this challenge in two ways. First, he may insist that God's reason does not flow from the divine nature, only that God possesses it and that it is in accordance with the divine nature. This response, however, raises the question concerning how God comes into possession of this reason to act. If God possesses this reason by neither logical nor natural necessity and there is nothing external to God that would cause him to have it, then it seems that God indeterminately possesses this reason. What then is the means by which God obtains this reason? He seems merely to assent to it for no reason, but this sort of assent would be pure reasonless whimsy on Helm's account. Since Helm cannot accept such indeterminism on the grounds that it is reasonless, he must hold that God's reason to act is natural and naturally necessitates him to act in a certain manner. This position contradicts his earlier claim that God does not act by natural necessity.

A second response that Helm might give is that while God's act of will is naturally necessitated, God himself is not a logically necessary being. Since God is not logically necessary, then fatalism is not necessarily true. Since God could fail to exist, his nature could fail to exist. If the divine nature fails to exist, then the world implied by the divine nature would also fail to exist. In this way, fatalism may be avoided. This response, however, is unsatisfactory. If God is a logically contingent being, then such a position implies that God could fail to exist. This raises the question concerning what determines whether or not God exists. If God can fail to exist, then something must determine whether or not God exists rather than not. Something determining whether or not God exists is absurd. God cannot determine that he exists for that would imply that he exists prior to existing, which is also absurd. Further, nothing is above God that determines that he exists; otherwise, God would not be God. He is the highest reality. Nothing is beyond him; therefore, Helm cannot claim that God is a logically contingent being. God must be a logically necessary being, and if he is logically necessary, then so is his nature and all that it implies. Since these responses do not hold up, Helm's view results in fatalism since the divine nature not only must exist but also must produce a certain world. This consequence is surely inimical to divine freedom.

A second issue with Helm's position is his conception of what constitutes free agency. For Helm, being logically and conceptually coherent is enough to make something logically possible. This statement is highly questionable because it assumes that, simply because God can conceive of a thing, it is something that he can actualize. This assumption appears to be far from the case. For example, God can coherently conceive of evil worlds and evil actions, but God cannot actualize such worlds and actions because of his perfect goodness. If God's nature necessitates him to choose to actualize a certain thing, then all other things, even if they are logically and conceptually coherent, will be logically impossible for God to actualize. As a result, the coherent conception of a thing does not seem to imply the logical possibility of a thing. The former is a matter of internal coherence. The latter is a matter of metaphysical existence. A thing may be internally coherent without being metaphysically possible.

Helm's assertion that a being is free if it has no external constraints is a contentious claim at best. While it is certainly true that a free being can have no external constraints, many hold that a free being must also have no internal constraints, such as one's nature of character. Compatibilists have long argued that free human agents need only avoid external constraints. While this position may prove true for human beings, it is questionable that it is true of God. As the divine being, it follows that God is free from external constraints on his being. As the highest reality, nothing outside of God can bind him and make him unfree. This fact, however, does not mean that no internal constraints within the divine being bind God and make him unfree. In fact, Helm's position appears to assert this. It requires internal constraints that necessitate that God act in a specific manner. While such necessity of human action would not imply fatalism, it would do so from a divine perspective. Since God is the highest reality, all things would be fated if he were internally constrained and not able to choose from a multiplicity of options. Once again, Helm's position appears to imply that fatalism is true and that logical possibility is ultimately false.

A final problem with Helm's position is his claim that the Thomistic position reduces divine choice to pure, reasonless whimsy. Helm's claim is strange given the fact that Aquinas openly states that God does not choose by reasonless whimsy. Aquinas is quite explicit in his claim that God acts to achieve his end, which is the divine goodness. This end or aim is God's reason for acting since it moves him to will; therefore, it does not appear to be true that God acts by reasonless whimsy in the Thomistic position. Helm might respond that while Aquinas acknowledges that God has a reason to act, God lacks a reason for acting in the manner that he does. As explained previously, Aquinas states that God must necessarily act in order to achieve his end, but the means by which God achieves that end are not necessary. God can choose among a number of options that would bring about his end. Helm might respond that such a choice of the means to the divine end is reasonless whimsy since God seems to choose arbitrarily which means to actualize rather than having a reasoned judgment.

This response, however, seems overblown. The fact that God can choose among options to achieve his divine end does not demonstrate that God's choice is devoid of reasoned judgment. Under the Thomistic position, God has a reason for acting but is free to choose the means to meet that end. As a result, the means must be in correspondence with but not determined by that end. God must reason as to what is the best means to obtain his end. No law of logic or nature dictates that he must choose one option over another, but God is free to reason as to which available option he prefers over the others. The availability of options requires that God utilize marginal utility to rationally select among alternatives. God reasons that certain outcomes are preferable to others in achieving the divine end. Such a selection is not reasonless but steeped in reason, even though it is indeterminate. In fact, Helm appears to imply this idea when he states that God does that which seems to him to be the best. If God does what seems to be the best, he seems to be acting indeterminately. Since there is no indication that what God chooses is certainly the best or that he must reason in this manner and to this end, then God's choice must be indeterminate because nothing determines that it is and must be the best option. God does have some level of indifference as to what he chooses since he is not required to choose it, and he is free to dispel that indifference via reasoned marginal judgment.

If this interpretation of Helm's statement is correct, then Helm's position is not only opposed to the Thomistic position as Helm states but it also appears that Helm's position is inconsistent with his own claim that God does not choose among options. Helm may mean that God's nature and character necessitate him to marginally choose a specific option because that option best fits the divine character. This interpretation, however, would lead back to fatalism and the loss of contingency, since God can choose no other than what his nature and character prescribes. Further, this interpretation does not fit Helm's use of language. To choose that which "seems" to be the best implies a lack of certainty and therefore a lack of knowledge. A God who acts according to the dictates of his nature or character cannot be said to lack certainty and knowledge about himself; therefore, Helm's claim implies indeterminacy and the ability to choose among options, making his overall position inconsistent.

As a result of the preceding discussion, Helm does not appear to present a viable alternative to the Thomistic position. His view implies the natural necessity he claims to reject. His definition of what constitutes contingency and free action does not square with the unique situation of the divine being as the highest reality. Finally, his claim that the indeterminacy of the Thomistic position implies reasonless whimsy is not evident, and his own position appears to imply the indeterminacy that he seeks to expunge. As a result, the Thomistic position on divine free action stands alone as the best available understanding of divine freedom.

Conclusion

In assessing the Atemporal Solution, not all atemporal views are compatible with a free God. There is, however, at least one position that is compatible and allows for a successful solution to the problem of foreknowledge and divine freedom. The logical moments framework in conjunction with a Thomistic position on divine action allows for God to be a free being. By nature, God seeks his own goodness which is his aim and the end for which he acts. Though God must necessarily act in order to obtain that end, the means by which he acts to achieve that end are not necessitated. He may freely and rationally choose among a number of options to achieve the divine end. As a result, God is libertarianly free in his act of will. Because God must seek his own goodness and because he is an atemporal being, this free act of will is essentially actualized in one atemporal moment. This act of will also produces a multiplicity of effects across the temporal world which are actualized at different temporal moments. As a result, God is able to know the entirety of his own life as well as the entire history of the world he has created.

This understanding of divine freedom can be conceptually understood according to three logical, non-temporal moments. The first logical moment consists of God's essential state of being and natural knowledge where God knows all that is logically possible. Logically flowing from that first moment, the second logical moment consists of God's free act of will. The act of will essentially flows from the divine nature though what is willed is contingent. Logically flowing from the second moment is the third logical moment which consists of God's free knowledge of his act of will and its effects. Thus, God moves in one atemporal instant from his essential state of being to his accidental state of being and gains knowledge in that atemporal movement. As a result, God is conditionally omniscient based upon his act of will as well as conditionally immutable and non-discursive in his accidental atemporal state of being. Thus, God does not lack knowledge or change at any moment in time although God does not essentially know his act of will and must obtain it.

Consequently, God's life is not determined and known logically prior to his act of will. Because God's life is open to real possibility, God is able to escape the threat of fatalism. Since God is able to freely choose the means by which he obtains his end, logical contingency and possibility are preserved. God's perfectly good nature does not necessitate him to will in a specific manner. Natural necessity does not apply to what God chooses; therefore, God is able to choose from among multiple alternatives that are compatible with God's goodness. Finally, the divine ideas do not pose a threat to the freedom of an atemporal God. In one atemporal act of will, God freely chooses to actualize all divine effects that are required to obtain a particular possible world. I conclude that the Thomistic logical moments framework of divine freedom meets all of the criteria for a successful solution to the problem of foreknowledge and divine freedom, and should be adopted over the rival theories.

Bibliography

Adams, Marilyn. "Is the Existence of God a 'Hard' Fact?" *PR* 76 (1967): 492–503.

———. *William Ockham*. Vol. 2. University of Notre Dame, 1987.

Adams, Robert. "An Anti-Molinist Argument." *PP* 5 (1991): 343–353.

———. *The Virtue of Faith and Other Essays in Philosophical Theology*. Oxford University Press, 1987.

Alston, William. "Divine Foreknowledge and Alternative Conceptions of Human Freedom." *IJPR* 18 (1985): 19–32.

———. *Divine Nature and Human Language: Essays in Philosophical Theology*. Cornell University Press, 1989.

Anselm. *St. Anselm: Basic Writings*. Translated by S. N. Deane. Open Court Publishing, 1968.

———. *De concordia praescientiae et praedestinationis et gratiae dei cum libero arbitrio*. In *Anselm of Canterbury*. Vol. 2. Edited and translated by Jasper Hopins and Herbert Richardson. Edwin Mellon Press, 1976.

Aquinas, Thomas. *Summa Contra Gentiles*. Vol. 1. Translated by Anton Pegis. University of Notre Dame Press, 1975.

———. *Summa Theologica*. Vol. 4. Translated by Blackfriars. McGraw-Hill Book Company, 1964.

———. *Truth*. Vol. 1. Translated by Robert Mulligan. Henry Regnery Company, 1952.

Augustine. *De Trinitate*. The Fathers of the Church 18. Translated by Stephen McKenna. Catholic University of America Press, 1963.

———. *Eighty-three Questions*. The Fathers of the Church 70. Translated by David Mosher. Catholic University of America Press, 1982.

———. *On Free Choice of the Will*. Translated by Anna Benjamin and L. H. Hackstaff. Prentice Hall, 1964.

Basinger, David. "Middle Knowledge and Classical Christian Thought." *RS* 22 (1986): 407–422.

———. "Middle Knowledge and Human Freedom: Some Clarifications." *FP* 4 (1987): 330–336.

———. "Omniscience and Deliberation: A Reply to Reichenbach." *IJPR* 20 (1986): 169–172.

———. *The Case for Freewill Theism*. InterVarsity, 1996.

Bave, Arvid. "A Deflationary Theory of Reference." *Synthese* 169 (2009): 51–73.

Bayliss, Charles. "Are Some Propositions Neither True Nor False?" *POS* 3 (1936): 156–166.

Bergmann, Michael and Jeffery Brower. "A Theistic Argument Against Platonism (and in Support of Truthmakers and Divine Simplicity)." Pages 357–386 in *Oxford Studies in Metaphysics*. Vol. 2. Edited by Dean Zimmerman. University of Oxford Press, 2006.

Bilezikian, Gilbert. *Christianity 101*. Zondervan, 1993.

Boehner, Philotheus. *Collected Articles on Ockham*. Edited by Eligius Buytaert. Franciscan Institute, 1958.

Boethius. *The Consolation of Philosophy*. Rev. ed. Translated by Victor Watts. Penguin, 1999.

Boyd, Gregory. "An Open Theism Response (to William Lane Craig)." Pages 144–148 in *Divine Foreknowledge: Four Views*. Edited by James Beilby and Paul Eddy. InterVarsity Press, 2001.

———. "Christian Love and Academic Dialog: a Reply to Bruce Ware." *JETS* 45 (2002): 233–243.

———. *God at War*. InterVarsity Press, 1997.

———. *God of the Possible*. Baker Books, 2000.

———. "God Limits His Control." Pages 183–208 in *Four Views on Divine Providence*. Edited by Stanley Gundry. Zondervan, 2011.

———. "Neo-Molinism and the Infinite Intelligence of God." *PC* 5 (2003): 187–204.

———. *Satan and the Problem of Evil*. InterVarsity Press, 2001.

———. "The Open Theism View." Pages 13–47 in *Divine Foreknowledge: Four Views*. Edited by James Beilby and Paul Eddy. InterVarsity Press, 2001.

———. "Two Ancient (and Modern) Motivations for Ascribing Exhaustively Definite Foreknowledge to God: A Historic Overview and Critical Assessment." *RS* 46 (2010): 41–59.

Chisholm, Roderick. "Knowledge and Belief: De Dicto and De Re." *PS* 29 (1976): 1–20.

Ciocchi, David. "The Religious Adequacy of Free-Will Theism." *RS* 38 (2002): 45–61.

Clouser, Roy. *The Myth of Religious Neutrality: An Essay on the Hidden Role of Religious Belief in Theories*. Rev. ed. University of Notre Dame Press, 2005.

Copan, Paul and William Lane Craig. *Creation Out of Nothing*. Baker Academic, 2004.

Copleston, Frederick. *A History of Philosophy*. Book 1. Vol. 2. Image Books, 1985.

Cowan, Steven. "The Grounding Objection to Middle Knowledge Revisited." *RS* 39 (2003): 93–102.

Cox, J. W. Roxbee. "Can I Know Beforehand What I Am Going to Decide?" *PR* 72 (1963): 88–92.

Craig, William Lane. "Anti-Platonism." Pages 113–126 in *Beyond the Control of God?: Six Views on the Problem of God and Abstract Objects*. Edited by Paul Gould. Bloomsbury, 2014.

———. "A Middle Knowledge Response (to Boyd)." Pages 55–60 in *Divine Foreknowledge: Four Views*. Edited by James Beilby and Paul Eddy. InterVarsity Press, 2001.

———. "A Nominalist Perspective on God and Abstract Objects." *PC* 13, no. 2 (2011): 305–318.

———. *Divine Foreknowledge and Human Freedom*. Brill, 1991.

———. "Ducking Friendly Fire: Davison on the Grounding Objection." *PC* 8 (2006): 161–166.

———. *God Over All: Divine Aseity and the Challenge of Platonism*. Oxford University Press, 2017.

———. "Middle Knowledge, Truth-Makers, and the "Grounding Objection"." *FP* 18 (2001): 337–352.

———. "Response to Gregory A. Boyd." Pages 224–230 in *Four Views on Divine Providence*. Edited by Stanley Gundry. Zondervan, 2011.

———. "Temporal Necessity: Hard Facts/Soft Facts." *IJPR* 20 (1986): 65–91.

———. *The Only Wise God*. Wipf and Stock, 1999.

———. *The Problem of Divine Foreknowledge and Future Contingents from Aristotle to Suarez*. Brill, 1988.

———. "The Tensed vs. Tenseless Theory of Time: A Watershed for the Conception of Divine Eternity." Pages 221–250 in *Questions of Time and Tense*. Edited by Robin Le Poidevin. Clarendon Press, 1998.

———. *Time and Eternity: Exploring God's Relationship to Time*. Crossway, 2001.

———. "What Does God Know?" Pages 137–156 in *God Under Fire*. Edited by Douglas Huffman and Eric Johnson. Zondervan, 2002.

———. "Why are (Some) Platonists So Insouciant?" *Philosophy* 86 (2011): 213–239.

Cross, Richard. "Gregory of Nyssa on Universals." *Vigiliae Christianae* 56 (2002): 372–410.

Davidson, Matthew. "A Demonstration Against Theistic Activism." *RS* 35 (1999): 277–290.

Davis, Richard. "God and the Platonic Horde: a Defense of Limited Conceptualism." *PC* 13, no. 2 (2011): 289–303.

———. *The Metaphysics of Theism and Modality*. Peter Land, 2001.

Davis, Stephen. *Logic and the Nature of God*. Eerdmans, 1983.

Davison, Scott. "Could Abstract Objects Depend Upon God?" *RS* 27 (1991): 485–497.

———. "Craig on the Grounding Objection to Middle Knowledge." *FP* 21 (2004): 365–369.

Dekker, Eef. "Explanatory Priority and Independence: On an Argument Against Middle Knowledge." *Sophia* 38 (1999): 1–14.

———. *Middle Knowledge*. Leuven: Peeters, 2000.

Descartes, Rene. *Oeuvres*. Edited by C. Adams and P. Tammery. Paris: Vrin, 1964.

———. *Philosophical Letters*. Translated by A. Kenny. Clarendon Press, 1970.

———. *Philosophical Works*. Translated by E. Haldane and G. T. Ross. Cambridge University Press, 1967.

DeWeese, Garrett. "Atemporal, Sempiternal, and Omnitemporal: God's Temporal Mode of Being." Pages 49–64 in *God and Time: Essays on the Divine Nature*. Edited by Gregory Ganssle and David Woodruff. Oxford University Press, 2002.

———. *God and the Nature of Time*. Ashgate, 2004.

Erickson, Millard. *God the Father Almighty*. Baker Books, 1998.

———. *What Does God Know and When Does He Know It?* Zondervan, 2003.

Felt, James. "God's Choice: Reflections on Evil in a Created World." *FP* 1 (1984): 370–377.

Fischer, John Martin. "Freedom and Foreknowledge." *PR* 92 (1983): 67–79.

———. "Hard-Type Soft Facts." *PR* 94 (1986): 591–601.

———. "Power Over the Past." *PPQ* 65 (1984): 335–350.

Flint, Thomas. *Divine Providence*. Cornell University Press, 1998.

Floyd, Graham. "*Imago Dei*: Why Christians Should Believe in Abstract Entities." Evangelical Philosophical Society. http://www.epsociety.org/userfiles/Graham%20Floyd-imago%20dei%20note%20final.pdf

Fouts, Avery. "Divine Self-Limitation in Swinburne's Doctrine of Omniscience." *RS* 29 (1993): 21–26.

Freddoso, Alfred. "Accidental Necessity and Logical Determinism." Pages 136–158 in *God, Foreknowledge, and Freedom*. Edited by John Martin Fisher. Stanford University Press, 1989.

———. "Accidental Necessity and Power Over the Past." *PPQ* 63 (1982): 54–68.

———. "Introduction." Pages 1–84 in Luis de Molina, *On Divine Foreknowledge: Part IV of the Concordia*. Translated by Alfred Freddoso. Cornell University Press, 1988.

Ganssle, Gregory, ed. *God and Time: Four Views*. InterVarsity, 2001.

Geach, Peter. *Providence and Evil*. Cambridge University Press, 1977.

Gettier, Edmund. "Is Justified True Belief Knowledge?" *Analysis* 23 (1963): 121–123.

Ginet, Carl. "Can the Will be Caused?" *PR* 71 (1962): 49–55.

Gordon, David and James Sadowsky. "Does Theism Need Middle Knowledge?" *RS* 25 (1989): 75–87.

Gould, Paul. "The Problem of God and Abstract Objects." *PC* 13, no. 2 (2011): 255–274.

———. "Theistic Activism: A New Problem and a New Solution." *PC* 13, no. 1 (2011): 127–139.

Gould, Paul and Richard Brian Davis. "Modified Theistic Activism." Pages 51–64 in *Beyond the Control of God?" Six Views on the Problem of God and Abstract Objects*. Edited by Paul Gould. Bloomsbury, 2014.

Grant, W. Matthews. "Can a Libertarian Hold That Our Free Acts are Caused by God?" *FP* 27 (2010): 22–44.

Grim, Patrick. "Against Omniscience: The Case from Essential Indexicals." *Nous* 9 (1985): 151–180.

Hasker, William. "A New Anti-Molinist Argument." *RS* 35 (1999): 291–297.

———. "A Refutation of Middle Knowledge." *Nous* 20 (1986): 545–557.

———. "Anti-Molinism is Undefeated!" *FP* 17 (2000): 126–131.

———. "A Philosophical Perspective." Pages 126–155 in *The Openness of God*. Clark Pinnock, et al. InterVarsity Press, 1994.

———. "Explanatory Priority: Transitive and Unequivocal, A Reply to William Craig." *PPR* 56 (1997): 389–393.

———. "Free Will Theism: A Reply to Ciocchi." *RS* 39 (2003): 431–440.

———. "God Takes Risks." Pages 218–228 in *Contemporary Debates in Philosophy of Religion*. Edited by Michael Peterson and Raymond VanArragon. Blackwell, 2004.

———. *God, Time, and Knowledge*. Cornell University Press, 1989.

———. "Hard Facts and Theological Fatalism." *Nous* 22 (1988): 419–436.

———. *Providence, Evil, and the Openness of God*. Routledge, 2004.

———. *The Triumph of God Over Evil*. InterVarsity Press, 2008.

———. "Yes, God has Beliefs!" *RS* 24 (1988): 385–394.
Hampshire, Stuart and H. L. A. Hart. "Decision, Intention, and Certainty." *Mind* 67 (1958): 1–12.
Helm, Paul. "Divine Foreknowledge and Facts." *CJP* 4 (1974): 305–315.
———. "Divine Timeless Eternity." Pages 28–60 in *God and Time*. Edited by Gregory Ganssle. InterVarsity Press, 2001.
———. *Eternal God*. Oxford University Press, 1988.
———. "Timelessness and Foreknowledge." *Mind* 84 (1975): 516–527.
Hess, Elijah. "Arguing from Molinism to Neo-Molinism." *PC* 17, no. 2 (2015): 331–351.
Hoffman, Joshua and Gary Rosenkrantz. "Hard and Soft Facts." *PR* 93 (1984): 419–434.
———. *The Divine Attributes*. Blackwell Publishing, 2002.
Jacobs, Nathan "On the Metaphysics of God and Creatures in the Eastern Pro-Nicenes." *PT* 28, no. 1 (2016): 3–42.
Jordan, Mark. "The Intelligibility of the World and the Divine Ideas in Aquinas." *RM* 38, no. 1 (1984): 17–32.
Kapitan, Tomis. "Can God Make Up His Mind?" *IJPR* 15 (1984): 37–47.
———. "Quantifying In." *Synthese* 29 (1968): 178–214.
Kenny, Anthony. "Freedom, Spontaneity, and Indifference." Pages 87–104 in *Essays on Freedom of Action*. Edited by Ted Honderich. Routledge and Kegan Paul, 1973.
———. *The God of the Philosophers*. Oxford University Press, 1979.
Koons, Robert. "Dual Agency: A Thomistic Account of Divine Providence and Human Freedom." *PC* 4 (2002): 397–410.
Koterski, Joseph. *An Introduction to Medieval Philosophy*. Wiley-Blackwell, 2009.
Kretzmann, Norman. "Omniscience and Immutability." *JP* 63 (1966): 409–421.
Kvanvig, Jonathan. *The Possibility of an All-Knowing God*. St. Martin's Press, 1986.
———. "Unknowable Truths and the Doctrine of Omniscience." *JAAR* 57 (1989): 485–508.
LaCroix, Richard. "Omniprescience and Divine Determinism." *RS* 12 (1976): 365–381.
Leff, Gordon. *William of Ockham*. Manchester University Press, 1975.
Leftow, Brian. "God and the Problem of Universals." Pages 325–356 in *Oxford Studies in Metaphysics*. Vol. 2. Edited by Dean Zimmerman. University of Oxford Press, 2006.
———. "Is God an Abstract Object?" *Nous* 24, no. 4 (1990): 581–598.
———. *Time and Eternity*. Cornell University Press, 1991.
Leibniz, G. W. *Discourse on Metaphysics and the Monadology*. Dover Philosophical Classics, 2005.
———. *Theodicy*. Edited by Austin Farrer. Translated by E. M. Huggard. Open Court, 1990.
Lewis, David. "Attitudes De Dicto and De Se." *PR* 88 (1979): 513–543.
Lucas, J. R. "Foreknowledge and the Vulnerability of God." Pages 119–128 in *The Philosophy in Christianity*. Edited by Godfrey Vesey. Cambridge University Press, 1989.
———. *Freedom and Grace*. Eerdmans, 1976.

———. *The Future*. Basil Blackwell, 1989.
MacGregor, Kirk. "The Neo-Molinist Square Collapses: A Molinist Response to Elijah Hess." *PC* 18, no. 1 (2016): 195–206.
Mann, William. "God's Freedom, Human Freedom, and God's Responsibility for Sin." Pages 182–210 in *Divine and Human Action*. Edited by Thomas Morris. Cornell University Press, 1988.
Martin, Aaron. "Reckoning with Ross: Possibles, Divine Ideas, and Virtual Practical Knowledge." *PACPA* 78 (2005): 193–208.
Mavrodes, George. "How Does God Know the Things He Knows?" Pages 345–361 in *Divine and Human Action*. Edited by Thomas Morris. Cornell University Press, 1988.
———. "Omniscience." Pages 236–242 in *A Companion to Philosophy of Religion*. Edited by Philip Quinn and Charles Taliaferro. Blackwell Publishers, 1997.
Mawson, T. J. "Divine Eternity." *IJPR* 64 (2008): 35–50.
McCann, Hugh. "Divine Sovereignty and the Freedom of the Will." *FP* 12 (1995): 582–598.
McTaggart, J. M. E. "The Unreality of Time." *Mind* 17 (1908): 457–473.
Menzel, Christopher. "Theism, Platonism, and the Metaphysics of Mathematics." *FP* 4, no. 4 (1987): 365–382.
Molina, Luis de. *On Divine Foreknowledge: Part IV of the Concordia*. Translated by Alfred Freddoso. Cornell University Press, 1988.
Morris, Thomas. *Anselmian Explorations*. University of Notre Dame Press, 1987.
———. *Our Idea of God*. University of Notre Dame Press, 1991.
Morriston, Wes. "Is God Free: Reply to Wierenga." *FP* 23 (2006): 93–98.
Murphree, John Tal. *Divine Paradoxes*. Christian Publications, 1998.
Normore, Calvin. "Divine Omniscience, Omnipotence, and Future Contingents: An Overview." Pages 3–22 in *Divine Omniscience and Omnipotence in Medieval Philosophy*. Edited by Tamar Rudavsky. D. Reidel, 1985.
O'Connor, Timothy. "The Impossibility of Middle Knowledge." *PS* 68 (1992): 139–166.
Ockham, William. *Predestination, God's Foreknowledge, and Future Contingents*. Translated by Marilyn Adams and Norman Kretzmann. Meredith Corporation, 1969.
———. *Quodlibeta Questions*, Vol. 1. Translated by Alfred Freddoso and Francis Kelly. Yale University Press, 1991.
Otte, Richard. "A Defense of Middle Knowledge." *IJPR* 21 (1987): 161–169.
Padgett, Alan. *God, Eternity, and the Nature of Time*. St. Martin's Press, 1992.
Pike, Nelson. "Divine Omniscience and Voluntary Action." *PR* 20 (1965): 27–46.
———. *God and Timelessness*. Routledge and Kegan Paul, 1970.
Pinnock, Clark. "Constrained by Love: Divine Self-Restraint According to Open Theism." *PRS* 34 (2007): 149–160.
———. "God Limits His Knowledge." Pages 141–162 in *Predestination and Free Will: Four Views on Divine Sovereignty and Human Freedom*. Edited by David and Randall Basinger. InterVarsity Press, 1986.

_____. *Most Moved Mover*. Baker Academic, 2001.

_____. "Open Theism: 'What is this? A new teaching?-and with authority!'" *ATJ* 34 (2003): 39–53.

Plantinga, Alvin. "Augustinian Christian Philosophy." *The Monist* 75, no. 3 (1992): 291–320.

_____. *Does God Have a Nature?* Marquette University Press, 2007.

_____. *God, Freedom, and Evil*. Eerdmans, 1974.

_____. "How to be an Anti-Realist." *PAAPA* 56, no. 1 (1982): 47–70.

_____. "Reason and Belief in God." Pages 16–93 in *Faith and Reason*. Edited by Alvin Plantinga and Nicholas Wolterstorff. University of Notre Dame Press, 1983.

_____. "Replies." In *Alvin Plantinga*. Edited by James Tomberlin and Peter van Inwagen. D. Reidel, 1985.

_____. *The Analytic Theist*. Edited by James Sennett. Eerdmans, 1998.

_____. *The Nature of Necessity*. Oxford, 1974.

Prior, A. N. "Formalities of Omniscience." In *Papers on Time and Tense*. Oxford University Press, 2003.

_____. *Papers on Time and Tense*. Clarendon Press, 1968.

_____. *Past, Present, and Future*. Oxford University Press, 1967.

Pseudo-Dionysius. *Divine Names*. Translated by C. E. Holt. Macmillan Company, 1940.

Purtill, Richard. "Fatalism and the Omnitemporality of Truth." *FP* 5 (1988): 185–192.

Quinn, Phillip. "Divine Foreknowledge and Divine Freedom." *IJPR* 9 (1978): 219–240.

Reichenbach, Bruce. "Omniscience and Deliberation." *IJPR* 16 (1984): 225–236.

Rhoda, Alan. "Generic Open Theism and Some Varieties Thereof." *RS* 44 (2008): 225–234.

Rhoda, Alan, Gregory Boyd, and Thomas Belt. "Open Theism, Omniscience, and the Nature of the Future." *FP* 23 (2006): 432–459.

Rice, Richard. "Divine Foreknowledge and Free Will." Pages 121–140 in *The Grace of God, the Will of Man*. Edited by Clark Pinnock. Zondervan, 1989.

_____. *God's Foreknowledge and Man's Free Will*. Bethany House Publishers, 1985.

Rizzler, James. "Open Theism: Does God Risk or Hope?" *RS* 42 (2006): 63–74.

Robinson, Michael. *Eternity and Freedom*. University Press of America, 1995.

Rogers, Katherin. *Perfect Being Theology*. Edinburgh University Press, 2000.

Rowe, William. *Can God Be Free?* Oxford University Press, 2004.

_____. *Philosophy of Religion: An Introduction*. 4th ed. Thomson and Wadsworth, 2007.

Sanders, John. "Be Wary of Ware: A Reply to Bruce Ware." *JETS* 45 (2002): 221–231.

_____. "God as Personal." Pages 165–80 in *The Grace of God, The Will of Man*. Edited by Clark Pinnock. Zondervan, 1989.

_____. "On Heffalumps and Heresies: Responses to Accusations Against Open Theism." *JBS* 2 (2002): 1–44.

_____. "Open Theism: Radical Revision or Miniscule Modification?" *WTJ* 38 (2001): 69–102.

_____. *The God Who Risks*. InterVarsity, 1998.

Saunders, John Turk. "Of God and Freedom." *PR* 75 (1966): 219–225.

———. "The Temptations of 'Powerlessness'." *APQ* 52 (1968): 100–108.

Shook, John. "God's Divinely Justified Knowledge is Incompatible with Human Free Will." *Forum Philosophicum: International Journal for Philosophy* 15 (2010): 141–159.

Smith, R. Scott. "Craig, Anti-Platonism, and Objective Morality." *PC* 19, no. 2 (2017): 331–343.

———."Craig's Nominalism and the High Cost of Preserving Divine Aseity." *EJPR* 9, no. 1 (2017): 87–107.

———. "William Lane Craig's Nominalism, Essences, and Implications for Our Knowledge of Reality." *PC* 15, no. 2 (2013): 365–382.

Sosa, E. "Consciousness of the Self and of the Present." Pages 131–147 in *Agent, Language, and Structure of the World*. Edited by J. Tomberlin. Hackett, 1983.

Stump, Eleonore. *Aquinas*. Routledge, 2003.

Suarez, Francisco. *Opera Omnia*. Edited by M. Andre and C. Brenton. Paris: Vives, 1956–78.

Sullivan, Thomas. "Omniscience, Immutability, and Divine Knowledge." *FP* 8 (1991): 21–35.

Swinburne, Richard. *The Christian God*. Oxford University Press, 1994.

———. *The Coherence of Theism*. Clarendon Press, 1977.

———. *The Coherence of Theism*. Rev. ed. Clarendon Press, 1993.

Talbott, Thomas. "On Divine Foreknowledge and Bringing About the Past." *PPR* 46 (1986): 455–469.

Taliaferro, Charles. "Divine Cognitive Power." *IJPR* 18 (1985): 133–140.

———. "Unknowable Truths and Omniscience: A Reply to Kvanvig." *JAAR* 61 (1993): 553–566.

Taylor, Richard. "Deliberation and Foreknowledge." *APQ* 1 (1964): 73–80.

Thomas, Mark. "Robert Adams and the Best Possible World." *FP* 13 (1996): 252–259.

Tooley, Michael. "Freedom and Foreknowledge." *FP* 17 (2000): 212–224.

Tuggy, Dale. "Three Roads to Open Theism." *FP* 24 (2007): 28–51.

Vallicella, William. "Divine Simplicity: A New Defense." *FP* 9 (1992): 508–552.

Van Inwagen, Peter. "A Theory of Properties." Pages 107–138 in *Oxford Studies in Metaphysics*. Vol. 1. Edited by Dean Zimmerman. Clarendon Press, 2004.

———. "God and Other Uncreated Things." Pages 3–20 in *Metaphysics and God: Essays in Honor of Eleonore Stump*. Edited by Kevin Timpe. Routledge, 2009.

———. "Relational vs. Constituent Ontologies." *PP* 25, no. 1 (2011): 389–405.

———. "Did God Create Shapes?" *PC* 17, no. 2 (2015): 285–290.

Welty, Greg. *Theistic Conceptual Realism: The Case for Interpreting Abstract Objects as Divine Ideas*. D.Phil. thesis, University of Oxford, 2006.

———. "Theistic Conceptual Realism." Pages 81–96 in *Beyond the Control of God?: Six Views on the Problem of God and Abstract Objects*. Edited by Paul Gould. Bloomsbury, 2014.

———. "Truth as Divine Ideas: A Theistic Theory of the Property 'Truth'." *SJT* 47, no. 1 (2004): 55–69.
Widerker, David. "Troubles with Ockhamism." *JP* 87 (1990): 462–480.
———. "Why God's Beliefs are Not Hard-Type Soft Facts." *RS* 38 (2002): 77–88.
Wierenga, Edward. "Omniscience." Pages 129–144 in *The Oxford Handbook of Philosophical Theology*. Edited by Thomas Flint and Michael Rea. Oxford University Press, 2009.
———. "The Freedom of God." *FP* 19 (2002): 425–436.
———. *The Nature of God*. Cornell University Press, 1989.
———. "Timelessness Out of Mind." Pages 153–164 *God and Time: Essays on the Divine Nature*. Edited by Gregory Ganssle and D. Woodruff. Oxford University Press, 2002.
Willard, Dallas. *The Divine Conspiracy*. Harper Collins, 1998.
Wolterstorff, Nicholas. "God Everlasting." Pages 181–203 in *God and the Good*. Edited by C. Orlebeke and L. Smeades. Eerdmans, 1975.
———. *On Universals*. University of Chicago Press, 1970.
Yandell, Keith. "God and Propositions." *PC* 13, no. 2 (2011): 275–287.
———. "God and Propositions." Pages 21–35 in *Beyond the Control of God?: Six Views on the Problem of God and Abstract Objects*. Edited by Paul Gould. Bloomsbury, 2014.
Yeats, John. *The Timelessness of God*. University Press of America, 1990.
Zagzebski, Linda. "Omniscience." Pages 261–270 in *The Routledge Companion to Philosophy of Religion*. Edited by Chad Meister and Paul Copan. Routledge, 2007.
———. "Omniscience, Time, and Freedom." Pages 3–25 in *The Blackwell Guide to Philosophy of Religion*. Edited by William Mann. Blackwell Publishing, 2005.
———. *The Dilemma of Freedom and Foreknowledge*. Oxford University Press, 1991.
Zemach, Eddy and David Widerker. "Facts, Freedom, and Foreknowledge." Pages 111–122 in *God, Foreknowledge, and Freedom*. Edited by John Martin Fischer. Stanford University Press, 1989.
Zhyrkova, Anna. "John Damascene's Notion of Being: Essence vs. Hypostical Existence." *SVTQ* 54 (2010): 85–105.